Rules Of Success

By
Onah Eje Johnbless

Unlocking the Secrets to Achieving True Success: The Golden Rules to Follow.

Table of Contents

Chapter 6
Resilience and Perseverance
- Understanding resilience
- Definition of resilience
- Why resilience is important for success
- Overcoming setbacks and failures
- Strategies for dealing with failure
- How to bounce back and persevere towards success
- Managing stress and handling pressure
- Techniques for managing stress
- Coping mechanisms for handling pressure in high-stress situations

Chapter 7
Adaptability and Flexibility
- Embracing change
- Importance of being adaptable in a constantly changing world
- Ways to practice adaptability
- Being open to new ideas and perspectives
- Benefits of being open-minded
- Techniques for being more open to new ideas and perspectives

- Problem-solving skills
- Strategies for effective problem-solving
- How to approach and overcome challenging situations

Chapter 8
Self-discipline and Accountability
- Understanding self-discipline
- Definition and importance of self-discipline
- Tips for developing self-discipline
- Holding oneself accountable
- Why accountability is important for success
- Ways to hold yourself accountable
- Avoiding procrastination
- Negative effects of procrastination
- Techniques for overcoming procrastination and staying focused

Chapter 9
Financial Management
- Importance of financial management
- Why financial stability is crucial for long-term success
- Principles for managing finances effectively

- *Investing for the future*
- *Understanding the importance of investing*
- *Strategies for making wise investments*
- *Budgeting and saving money*
- *Styles for creating and sticking to a budget*
- *Part ways to save money for future goals and investments*

Chapter 10
Leadership Skills
- *Characteristics of effective leaders*
- *Key traits of successful leaders*
- *How to develop and strengthen leadership skills*
- *Delegating tasks and empowering others*
- *Importance of delegation in effective leadership*
- *Tips for delegating tasks and empowering team members*
- *Conflict resolution*
- *Strategies for resolving conflicts and promoting a positive work environment*

- Communication techniques for handling difficult situations

Chapter 11
Continuous self-improvement
- Importance of continuous self-improvement
- Why it is crucial to keep striving for personal growth?
- Ways to continuously improve oneself
- Seeking guidance and mentorship
- Benefits of having a mentor or coach
- How to find and learn from mentors
- Celebrating and learning from failures and successes
- Understanding the importance of reflection and learning from experiences
- How to use failures and successes as opportunities for growth

Chapter 12 Conclusion
- Recap of the rules of success
- Encouragement to implement these rules in daily life
- Final thoughts on achieving success.

Copyright

Preface

Success is a universal goal that we all strive for in our lives, whether it be in our personal or professional endeavors. We all dream of achieving great things, but often find ourselves falling short and wondering what we could have done differently. This led me on a journey to discover what sets successful individuals apart from the rest.

After years of extensive research and study, I have compiled a set of rules that have proven to be the pillars of success for countless individuals throughout history. These rules are not a quick-fix solution or a magic formula, but rather a comprehensive guide that will help you lay a solid foundation for achieving your goals and reaching your full potential.

The "Rules of Success" are not limited to any specific field or area of life, but rather apply to all aspects. Whether you are a student, an entrepreneur, an athlete, or simply someone looking to improve their life, these rules will provide you with invaluable insights and practical advice.

This book aims to inspire and motivate readers to take control of their lives and pursue their dreams with determination and perseverance. It contains powerful lessons and real-life examples that will demonstrate the impact of these rules and offer guidance on how to apply them in your own life.

I must emphasize that success is not a one-size-fits-all concept. Different people have different definitions of success, and the path to achieving it may vary. However, these rules have stood the test of time and have been proven to be essential for anyone looking to achieve their version of success.

I hope this book will serve as a valuable resource and guide on your journey towards success. It is my sincere belief that by following these rules, you will be able to unlock your full potential and live a fulfilling and successful life. Remember, success is not a destination; it is a continuous journey of growth and learning.

I would like to end this preface with a quote by Jack Canfield, "Success is not a matter of luck, it's a matter of doing the right things consistently and letting the results take care of themselves." May these rules help you in doing the right things consistently and pave the way for your success.

Best of luck on your journey!

Onah Eje Johnbless

Introduction

Definition of success

Success can be defined as the achievement of a desired goal or outcome. It is the realization of one's aspirations and the fulfillment of one's potential. Success is a subjective concept that differs from person to person, as everyone has their own set of goals and objectives. It is not a one-size-fits-all concept and cannot be measured by a single standard.

Success is often associated with wealth, fame, and power, but it is not limited to these external factors. True success is a combination of personal growth, contentment, happiness, and a sense of fulfillment. It is a journey of self-discovery and constant improvement, rather than a destination.

One of the key characteristics of success is perseverance. It is the determination to overcome challenges and obstacles that come in the way of achieving one's goals. A successful person is willing to put in the hard work, make sacrifices, and face failures, knowing that they will eventually lead to success.

Success is also closely linked with passion and self-belief. A person who is passionate about their goals, and believes in their abilities, is more likely to achieve success than someone who lacks motivation and self-confidence. It is the positive mindset and the belief in one's potential that drives a person towards success.

Moreover, success is not achieved overnight. It is a gradual process that requires patience, dedication, and perseverance. It also involves taking risks and stepping out of one's comfort zone. Success is not possible without embracing and learning from failures and setbacks. It is important to view failures as opportunities for growth and use them as stepping stones towards success.

It is worth noting that success does not exist in isolation. It is often a result of collaboration, mentorship, and support from others. Successful individuals acknowledge the importance of a network and relationships in their journey towards success. They also give back and use their success to inspire and help others achieve their goals.

Ultimately, success goes beyond material possessions and achievements. It is a state of mind and a feeling of contentment. It is when a person can look back at their journey and feel proud of the obstacles they have overcome, the goals they have achieved, and the impact they have made. Success is a continuous and ever-evolving process that requires lifelong learning, growth, and fulfillment.

Importance of success

Success is often defined as the accomplishment of one's goals or the attainment of prosperity and recognition. It is a desired outcome that everyone aspires to achieve in one form or another. Whether it is in our personal or professional lives, success holds significant meaning and importance. In this modern, fast-paced world, where competition is high, the pursuit of success has become more critical than ever. Here are some of the reasons why success is crucial.

Motivation and Fulfillment: One of the main reasons why success is essential is that it acts as a source of motivation. When we have a goal in mind and work towards achieving it, the sense of accomplishment and fulfillment we get upon achieving it is unbeatable. This sense of achievement keeps us motivated to do better and strive for even more significant success.

Self-Confidence and Self-Esteem: Success plays a crucial role in building our self-confidence and self-esteem. When we achieve something we have been working hard for, it boosts our belief in our abilities and ourselves. This confidence, in turn, leads to an increase in our self-esteem, a belief in our value and worth as a person.

Financial Stability: Another crucial aspect of success is financial stability and security. In today's world, money is an essential factor in determining our standard of living. Success in our careers or businesses ensures a stable and secure financial future for ourselves and our loved ones.

Respect and Recognition: Success comes with respect and recognition from others. When we achieve our goals, people admire and acknowledge our efforts, which in turn boosts our self-esteem. Moreover, success brings with it a sense of accomplishment and pride, making us feel valued and recognized.

Personal Growth and Development: Working towards success requires us to push our boundaries, learn new things and develop ourselves personally and professionally. This constant growth and development help us become better versions of ourselves, both personally and in our careers.

Opportunities and Choices: Success opens doors and provides us with endless opportunities and choices to explore. It allows us to choose the path we want to take and make decisions that align with our goals and aspirations. With success comes the freedom to choose and the ability to shape our future.

Impact on Others: Success not only benefits us but also impacts the people around us positively. Our achievements inspire and motivate others to strive for success and brings happiness and positivity to our loved ones. In this way, our success can create a ripple effect and make a difference in the lives of others.

Inner Satisfaction and Happiness: Ultimately, success brings a sense of inner satisfaction and happiness that cannot be replicated by any material possession. The satisfaction of knowing that we have achieved our goals and that our hard work has paid off is unparalleled. It brings a sense of peace, contentment, and happiness that money cannot buy.

Success holds immense importance in our lives. It serves as a driving force, a source of motivation and fulfillment, and a symbol of personal growth and development. It impacts us and those around us positively and brings a sense of inner satisfaction and happiness. Therefore, it is crucial to set goals and work towards achieving them, as success can transform our lives in ways we never thought possible.

Purpose of the rules of success

The purpose of the rules of success is to provide individuals with a set of guidelines and principles that can help them achieve their goals and aspirations. These rules serve as a roadmap to success, laying out the necessary steps and actions that individuals can take to reach their desired level of success.

One of the main purposes of the rules of success is to provide individuals with a clear understanding of what success looks like and how to attain it. Many people have different interpretations of success and may struggle to define it for themselves. These rules serve as a universal definition of success that can guide individuals towards achieving their own specific versions of it.

The rules of success also serve as a source of motivation and inspiration. They highlight the qualities and habits that successful people possess, such as determination, discipline, and perseverance. By following these rules, individuals can adopt these qualities and apply them to their own lives, thus increasing their chances of success.

Another important purpose of the rules of success is to provide individuals with a sense of direction and focus. Without a clear set of guidelines, individuals may feel lost or unsure of which path to take to achieve their goals. The rules of success act as a compass, helping individuals stay on track and make the right decisions to progress towards their goals.

The rules of success also serve as a tool for personal growth and development. Success is not just about achieving external goals; it is also about constantly evolving and improving as a person. By following these rules, individuals can learn valuable lessons about self-discipline, self-reflection, and continuous improvement.

Furthermore, the rules of success promote a positive mindset and a can-do attitude. Many of these rules emphasize the power of positive thinking and the importance of believing in oneself. By practicing these principles, individuals can overcome self-doubt and develop a mindset that is conducive to success.

In addition, the rules of success instill a sense of responsibility and accountability. Success is not handed to individuals on a silver platter; it requires hard work, determination, and responsibility. These rules encourage individuals to take ownership of their actions and decisions, and to hold themselves accountable for the results.

Lastly, the purpose of the rules of success is to create a better and more successful society. When individuals are successful, they can make positive contributions to their communities and the world at large. By following these rules, individuals can not only achieve personal success but also make a positive impact on others and society.

The rules of success serve as a guide, a motivator, a source of direction, personal growth, and societal improvement. They provide individuals with the tools and principles needed to turn their dreams into reality. By following these rules, individuals can unlock their full potential and live a successful and fulfilling life.

Chapter 1
Personal Development

A. Mindset

Personal development is the continuous and intentional process of improving oneself through self-reflection, self-awareness, and the acquisition of new knowledge, skills, and experiences. It is a journey towards becoming the best version of oneself, both personally and professionally, and achieving a fulfilling and meaningful life.

At the core of personal development lies mindset - one's beliefs, attitudes, and thoughts that shape their behavior, actions, and reactions to different situations in life. It is the foundation upon which personal growth and development are built. In other words, mindset is the lens through which one views and interprets the world.

There are two main types of mindset - a fixed mindset and a growth mindset. A fixed mindset is one in which a person believes that their abilities, intelligence, and talents are fixed traits and cannot be changed. In contrast, a growth mindset is one in which individuals believe that their intelligence, abilities, and talents can be developed and improved upon through effort, persistence, and learning.

Now, the question arises, why is mindset so crucial in personal development? Firstly, mindset is closely associated with one's self-esteem and self-belief. A person with a fixed mindset typically has lower self-esteem and is less likely to take risks, try new things, and push themselves out of their comfort zone. On the other hand, someone with a growth mindset is more likely to have a positive self-image and believe in their ability to overcome challenges and achieve their goals.

Secondly, mindset plays a significant role in shaping one's mindset towards failure and success. A person with a fixed mindset tends to view failure as a reflection of their abilities and give up easily when faced with obstacles. In contrast, someone with a growth mindset sees failure as an opportunity to learn and improve, and they are more resilient in the face of challenges.

Moreover, mindset also affects one's attitude towards lifelong learning and personal growth. Individuals with a fixed mindset often believe that their intelligence and abilities are predetermined and that there is little room for improvement. As a result, they are less likely to continue learning and developing new skills. In contrast, individuals with a growth mindset see learning as a lifelong journey, and they are open to new experiences and challenges that allow them to grow and evolve.

Developing a growth mindset is crucial for personal development and achieving one's full potential. One can cultivate a growth mindset by challenging negative thought patterns, embracing failures and setbacks as opportunities for growth, and seeking out new challenges and learning opportunities. Additionally, surrounding oneself with positive and supportive individuals and seeking encouragement and feedback can also aid in developing a growth mindset.

One's mindset is a critical factor in personal development as it shapes one's attitude, actions, and beliefs. By cultivating a growth mindset, individuals can shift their perspective to view challenges as opportunities, believe in their abilities to learn and grow, and continue developing themselves for a fulfilling and successful life.

Importance of positive mindset

Having a positive mindset is crucial in today's fast-paced and competitive world. It refers to having an optimistic outlook and attitude towards life, even in the face of challenges and obstacles. A positive mindset allows individuals to focus on the good in every situation, leading to overall happiness and success. It is not just a personality trait but a learned skill that can be cultivated and nurtured through self-awareness and daily practices.

One of the main benefits of a positive mindset is its impact on one's mental health. Individuals with a positive mindset are less likely to experience anxiety, stress, and depression. They are better equipped to tackle life's curveballs and bounce back from setbacks. This is because they have a better perspective on the situation, and they believe that they have the strength and ability to overcome any obstacle that comes their way.

Moreover, positive thinking has a direct impact on one's physical health. Studies have shown that individuals with a positive mindset have stronger immune systems, lower blood pressure, and a reduced risk of developing cardiovascular diseases. This is because a positive mindset helps in managing stress levels, which can have detrimental effects on physical health.

Furthermore, having a positive mindset can also lead to increased productivity and success. People with a positive mindset tend to be more motivated, focused, and resilient in pursuing their goals. They are not discouraged by failures and setbacks but use them as learning opportunities to improve and move forward. This attitude translates into higher levels of productivity and success in both personal and professional life.

Having a positive mindset also greatly impacts one's relationships and social interactions. People with a positive outlook tend to attract like-minded individuals and build strong and supportive relationships. They are more empathetic towards others and have better communication skills, which helps them maintain healthy and fulfilling relationships.

In addition to personal benefits, having a positive mindset can also have a ripple effect on society. Positive individuals radiate positivity, which can be contagious. This can create a positive and uplifting environment, not just for themselves but for those around them. It can improve the overall mood and attitude of a community, leading to a more harmonious and supportive society.

In contrast, individuals with a negative mindset tend to have a defeatist attitude. They view challenges as insurmountable and often blame external factors for their failures. This negative thinking can hold them back from achieving their full potential and hinder their personal growth and development. It can also lead to a negative and toxic environment, affecting not just their own well-being but also those around them.

The importance of a positive mindset cannot be overstated. It is a key factor in leading a fulfilling and successful life. By cultivating a positive mindset, one can achieve a healthier state of mind, improved physical health, increased productivity and success, and stronger relationships. It is a powerful tool that can help individuals navigate through life's challenges and ultimately achieve their goals and dreams.

Techniques to develop a positive mindset

Developing a positive mindset is crucial for living a healthy and fulfilling life. It involves changing our patterns of thinking and behavior to focus on the positive aspects of ourselves, others, and our surroundings. However, maintaining a positive mindset can be challenging as we are constantly bombarded with negative influences from the media, daily stressors, and our own inner critical voice. But with deliberate effort and practice, we can develop techniques to cultivate a positive mindset.

Practice Gratitude

Gratitude is the act of appreciating and being thankful for what we have in our lives. When we focus on what we are grateful for, we shift our mindset from one of lack and negativity to abundance and positivity. This can be done through keeping a gratitude journal, where we write down things that we are thankful for each day. By acknowledging and being grateful for the good in our lives, we train our minds to see the positive instead of dwelling on the negative.

Positive Self-Talk

The way we talk to ourselves has a significant impact on our mindset. Negative self-talk can be damaging as it reinforces limiting beliefs and lowers self-esteem. On the other hand, positive self-talk can do wonders for our mindset, helping us to build self-confidence and resilience. One way to cultivate positive self-talk is by using affirmations. These are positive statements that we repeat to ourselves daily to counter any negative thoughts. For example, "I am capable and deserving of success" or "I am an optimistic and resilient person."

Surround Yourself with Positive People

The people we spend most of our time with can heavily influence our mindset. It is essential to surround ourselves with positive and supportive individuals who uplift us and believe in our abilities. Spending time with people who have a positive mindset can also help us see things from a different perspective and give us motivation and inspiration to stay positive.

Focus on Solutions

When facing challenges or setbacks, it is easy to get caught up in negative thinking or blaming others for our circumstances. However, a positive mindset involves shifting our focus to finding solutions rather than dwelling on problems. By looking for ways to overcome obstacles and learn from our experiences, we develop a resilient and optimistic mindset.

Take Care of Your Physical and Mental Well-being

Our physical and mental health greatly affects our mindset. When we are tired, stressed, or unhealthy, it can be challenging to maintain a positive outlook on life. Therefore, it is crucial to prioritize self-care by getting enough rest, exercising regularly, and practicing mindfulness and relaxation techniques. These activities can help reduce stress and promote a positive mindset.

Set Realistic Goals

Setting achievable goals and working towards them can boost our self-esteem and sense of purpose, leading to a positive mindset. It is essential to set realistic goals that align with our values and interests. Instead of focusing on perfection, we should celebrate our progress and efforts towards our goals, even if we experience setbacks along the way.

Learn from Rejections and Failures

Failure and rejection are inevitable in life, and they can cause us to have a negative mindset. However, we can use these experiences as opportunities for growth and learning. Rather than dwelling on our mistakes, we can reflect on them and find ways to improve. This can help us build resilience and a positive attitude towards future challenges.

In conclusion, developing a positive mindset is an ongoing process that requires conscious effort and practice. By incorporating these techniques into our daily lives, we can train our minds to see the good in ourselves and our surroundings, leading to a happier and more fulfilling life.

Self-awareness

Self-awareness is a quintessential element of human consciousness that involves the ability to understand one's thoughts, feelings, and behavior. It is the conscious knowledge and recognition of one's own existence, character, emotions, desires, and limitations. Essentially, it refers to having a deep understanding of oneself, including one's strengths and weaknesses, values, beliefs, and motivations.

Self-awareness is a crucial aspect of personal development and plays a vital role in shaping an individual's personality and behavior. It allows people to introspect, reflect, and gain insight into their thoughts, emotions, and actions, which ultimately leads to self-discovery and growth.

One of the key components of self-awareness is introspection, which involves actively questioning and examining one's own thoughts, feelings, and behaviors. This process allows individuals to gain a deeper understanding of themselves, their thought processes, and the reasons behind their actions.

Another crucial aspect of self-awareness is self-exploration, which involves exploring one's interests, values, and passions. It enables individuals to identify their strengths and weaknesses and make informed decisions about their personal and professional lives. Additionally, self-exploration can also help individuals understand their goals and priorities, guiding them towards a fulfilling and meaningful life.

Self-awareness also involves recognizing and regulating one's emotions. Emotions are an essential aspect of the human experience, and being aware of them can help individuals understand how they are feeling and why. By being aware of their emotions, individuals can manage them better and respond to situations in a more rational and constructive manner.

Moreover, self-awareness also allows individuals to understand the impact of their actions on others. By being mindful of their behavior, individuals can develop empathy and consider others' perspectives, leading to improved relationships and communication.

Having a high level of self-awareness also enables individuals to recognize their biases and prejudices. It helps in gaining a better understanding of one's own beliefs and values and how they may influence one's perceptions and actions towards others.

Self-awareness is not only essential for personal development but also for success in various areas of life. People who possess exceptional self-awareness are more likely to set realistic goals, make informed decisions, and take responsibility for their actions. They are also better at managing stress, building healthy relationships, and adapting to changing situations.

In contrast, a lack of self-awareness can lead to a variety of negative consequences. It can result in difficulty in managing emotions, making poor decisions, and having conflicts in relationships. It can also hinder personal growth and limit an individual's potential.

In today's fast-paced world, where distractions are abundant, and people are more focused on external factors, developing self-awareness has become more critical than ever. It requires conscious effort, introspection, and an open mind. Some of the ways to cultivate self-awareness include mindfulness practices, keeping a journal, seeking feedback from others, and reflective thinking.

Self-awareness is a fundamental aspect of human consciousness that allows individuals to understand and accept themselves fully. It facilitates personal growth and leads to a more fulfilling and successful life. By being self-aware, individuals can foster a deeper connection with themselves and live a more authentic and purposeful life.

Understanding strengths and weaknesses

Understanding our strengths and weaknesses is a crucial aspect of personal growth and development. It allows us to recognize our areas of expertise and areas in which we need improvement, leading to more effective decision making and increased self-awareness.

Strengths can be defined as the unique qualities and abilities that come naturally to us. They are the traits that make us stand out and excel in certain areas. These can be traits such as leadership, creativity, empathy, or problem-solving skills. Identifying our strengths helps us build confidence and capitalize on our talents to achieve our goals and aspirations.

On the other hand, weaknesses are the limitations or areas where we struggle. They can be either skills or personal characteristics that hinder our progress. Weaknesses can be manifested as lack of organization, poor time management, or difficulty in dealing with criticism. Understanding our weaknesses helps us identify where we need to improve and take steps towards self-improvement.

One of the main challenges in understanding our strengths and weaknesses lies in self-awareness. It is often difficult for individuals to accurately assess their own abilities, as our perceptions can be clouded by biases and subjective judgments. This is where feedback and assessment from others can be beneficial. Seeking feedback from peers, colleagues, and mentors can provide valuable insights into our strengths and areas for improvement.

Self-reflection is another powerful tool in understanding our strengths and weaknesses. Taking time to reflect on our experiences, actions, and reactions can provide insights into our behaviors and thought patterns. Journaling or seeking therapy can also aid in this process, as it allows us to explore our thoughts and feelings in a safe and non-judgmental space.

Another useful approach to understanding our strengths and weaknesses is through self-assessment tools and tests. These tests, such as the Myers-Briggs Type Indicator or the StrengthsFinder, provide a structured way to identify our personality traits and natural abilities. These tools can help individuals gain a better understanding of themselves and assess their strengths and weaknesses objectively.

Once we have a clear understanding of our strengths and weaknesses, it is essential to develop a plan to utilize our strengths and work on our weaknesses. Leveraging our strengths allows us to increase our productivity, happiness, and success in various areas of our lives. On the other hand, recognizing our weaknesses allows us to take actionable steps towards self-improvement and personal growth.

It is crucial to remember that our strengths and weaknesses are not fixed and can change over time. Life experiences, learning opportunities, and personal growth can all impact our strengths and weaknesses. Therefore, it is essential to regularly reassess and update our understanding of ourselves.

Understanding our strengths and weaknesses is a continual process that requires self-reflection, feedback from others, and assessment tools. It helps us make better decisions, develop self-awareness, and reach our full potential. By embracing our strengths and working on our weaknesses, we can lead more fulfilling and successful lives.

Strategies to improve self-awareness

Self-awareness is the ability to understand one's own thoughts, emotions, and behaviors, and how they influence one's actions and interactions with others. It is an important aspect of personal growth and development and can lead to increased confidence, better decision-making, and improved relationships. However, it is not something that comes naturally to everyone and may need to be actively developed. Here are some strategies to improve self-awareness:

Practice introspection: Introspection is the process of looking inward and examining one's thoughts and feelings. It involves paying attention to your inner dialogue, discovering your values and beliefs, and understanding how they impact your behavior. Take time to reflect on your thoughts, emotions, and experiences on a regular basis. Keeping a journal can be a helpful tool in this process.

Seek feedback: Another effective way to increase self-awareness is to seek feedback from others. Ask trusted friends, family members, or colleagues for their honest opinions about your strengths and weaknesses. This feedback can help you gain a different perspective and identify blind spots that you may not be aware of.

Be mindful: Mindfulness is the practice of being fully present in the moment, without judgment. It can help you become more aware of your thoughts, emotions, and behaviors. Mindfulness techniques such as deep breathing, meditation, and body scan can help you tune in to your internal experiences and become more self-aware.

Learn from your mistakes: Making mistakes is inevitable, but what matters is what we learn from them. Take the time to reflect on your mistakes and understand what went wrong and why. This can help you gain insight into your patterns of behavior and make changes for the future.

Engage in self-reflection: Self-reflection is the process of looking back on your experiences and evaluating your thoughts, feelings, and behaviors. It can help you understand yourself better and gain a deeper understanding of your motivations and behaviors.

Try new things: Sometimes, we may get stuck in our comfort zone and fail to challenge ourselves. Trying new things, whether it's a new hobby, skill, or experience, can help you discover new aspects of yourself and increase your self-awareness.

Seek professional help: If you find it challenging to improve your self-awareness on your own, seeking the help of a therapist or counselor can be beneficial. They can provide an objective perspective and guide you in developing self-awareness through various techniques such as cognitive-behavioral therapy, mindfulness-based therapy, and more.

Embrace your emotions: Emotions are a natural part of being human, and it's essential to acknowledge and express them. Avoid suppressing your emotions and try to understand their underlying causes. This can help you become more aware of your triggers and how you react to them.

Embrace feedback: Feedback, whether positive or negative, can be valuable in increasing self-awareness. Instead of getting defensive or taking it personally, try to listen to feedback objectively and use it as a tool for self-reflection and growth.

Self-awareness is a continuous process that requires effort and intention. By incorporating these strategies into your daily life, you can increase your self-awareness and gain a deeper understanding of yourself, leading to personal growth and improvement. Remember that self-awareness is a journey, not a destination, and it will continue to evolve as you grow and learn.

Continuous learning

Continuous learning refers to the process of constantly acquiring new knowledge, skills, and behaviors throughout one's lifetime to enhance personal and professional growth. It is a proactive approach to learning that goes beyond the traditional education system and extends into the day-to-day activities of an individual.

In today's fast-paced and ever-changing world, continuous learning has become a crucial aspect of personal and professional development. With advancements in technology, industries are evolving at a rapid pace, and new skills are in demand. Therefore, it is essential for individuals to continuously update their knowledge and skills to remain relevant in their fields and stay ahead of the competition.

Continuous learning can take many forms, such as attending workshops, seminars, conferences, and online courses. It can also be achieved through self-directed learning, where individuals take the initiative to learn new skills and acquire knowledge in their free time. Additionally, on-the-job training, job rotations, and mentoring programs can also contribute to continuous learning.

One of the main benefits of continuous learning is that it helps individuals adapt to change and embrace new challenges. With a rapidly changing job market, it is crucial for individuals to continuously update their skills and knowledge to remain competitive.

Continuous learning enables individuals to stay open-minded, flexible, and adaptable to new situations and changes.

Moreover, continuous learning also leads to personal and professional growth. As individuals acquire new skills and knowledge, they become more valuable to their employers, leading to better job prospects and career opportunities. Continuous learning also helps individuals to become more efficient and effective in their current roles, which can lead to increased job satisfaction and better job performance.

Another significant advantage of continuous learning is that it can broaden an individual's perspective and promote critical thinking. By learning new things and exposing oneself to different ideas and perspectives, individuals can enhance their problem-solving skills, creativity, and decision-making abilities. This can be especially beneficial in the workplace, where individuals are constantly faced with new challenges and complex tasks.

Continuous learning also contributes to personal development and self-improvement. It allows individuals to identify their strengths and weaknesses and work on improving them to reach their full potential. It can also help individuals to discover new interests and passions, leading to a more fulfilled and enriching life.

Furthermore, continuous learning is essential for keeping up with advancements in technology. In today's digital age, technology is constantly evolving, and individuals need to continuously update their skills to keep up with the latest trends. Continuous learning can help individuals to understand and utilize new technologies in their personal and professional lives efficiently.

Continuous learning is a crucial aspect of personal and professional development in the modern world. It enables individuals to remain relevant, adaptable, and valuable in the job market, promotes personal growth and self-improvement, and broadens their perspectives and critical thinking abilities. Therefore, it is essential for individuals to adopt a mindset of continuous learning and make it a lifelong habit.

Importance of lifelong learning

Lifelong learning refers to the continuous process of acquiring knowledge, skills, and attitudes throughout one's life. It goes beyond the formal education system and includes various forms of learning such as self-directed learning, informal learning, and even on-the-job training. In today's rapidly changing world, the concept of lifelong learning has become increasingly important and necessary. It is no longer enough to simply acquire a degree or certification and consider one's education complete. Instead, individuals must embrace the idea of lifelong learning in order to thrive in both their personal and professional lives.

The importance of lifelong learning can be seen in various aspects of life. First and foremost, it allows individuals to stay relevant and adapt to the constantly evolving job market. With the rapid advancements in technology and automation, many jobs are becoming obsolete while new ones are emerging. Lifelong learning enables individuals to develop new skills and knowledge that are in demand, making them valuable and competitive in the job market. This not only increases their chances of employability but also opens up opportunities for career advancement and higher salaries.

Moreover, lifelong learning has a significant impact on personal growth and development. It provides individuals with opportunities to explore new interests and passions, promoting self-discovery and fulfillment. The continuous pursuit of knowledge also helps to expand one's perspective and understanding of the world, enhancing critical thinking and problem-solving skills. This, in turn, leads to personal growth and a sense of purpose, which are crucial for overall well-being and happiness.

Lifelong learning also plays a vital role in maintaining mental health and cognitive abilities. Studies have shown that engaging in mental activities such as learning new skills and acquiring knowledge can help prevent cognitive decline and improve memory. As individuals age, lifelong learning can help keep the mind sharp and active, promoting a sense of accomplishment and satisfaction.

In addition to personal growth, lifelong learning has a positive impact on society as a whole. As individuals continue to develop new skills and knowledge, they contribute to the growth and development of their communities and society. They become more informed and engaged citizens, who are better equipped to address social issues and contribute to the betterment of their communities.

Furthermore, lifelong learning promotes a culture of continuous improvement and innovation. It encourages individuals and organizations to seek new ways of doing things and embrace change. As a result, this fosters creativity and innovation, leading to advancements in various fields and industries.

In today's globalized world, where knowledge and technology are constantly evolving, the importance of lifelong learning cannot be overstated. It is essential for individuals to stay competitive, adapt to change, and lead fulfilling lives. Governments and organizations also have a crucial role to play in promoting lifelong learning by providing opportunities for individuals to access education and training throughout their lives.

Lifelong learning is crucial for personal growth, professional development, and societal progress. It allows individuals to stay relevant, adapt to change, maintain cognitive abilities, and contribute to their communities. Therefore, it is important for individuals to embrace the concept of lifelong learning and make it a lifelong commitment to continuous growth and development.

Ways to stay educated and up-to-date

In today's fast-paced and constantly changing world, it is essential to stay educated and up-to-date to ensure personal and professional growth. With the advent of technology and increased access to information, there are several ways to stay informed and knowledgeable about various subjects. In this essay, we will discuss elaborately on the ways to stay educated and up-to-date.

Read books and articles: Reading is one of the most effective ways to expand knowledge and stay updated on various topics. Books and articles written by experts in their fields provide in-depth information, insights, and perspectives on a subject. With the rise of e-books and online articles, it is easier than ever to access a vast range of reading material from anywhere in the world. To stay updated and educated, it is important to read a variety of genres, including non-fiction, self-help, and current affairs.

Attend workshops and seminars: Another way to stay educated and up-to-date is by attending workshops and seminars. They offer a great opportunity to learn from experienced professionals, network with like-minded individuals, and gain new perspectives on a subject. With the advent of virtual workshops and webinars, attending such events has become more easily accessible and convenient. These events also offer hands-on learning experiences, making it easier to grasp complex concepts.

Enroll in online courses: The rise of online learning platforms has made it possible for individuals to access quality education from the comfort of their homes. There are various online courses available on a diverse range of topics, from business and finance to coding and design. These courses are often taught by industry experts and provide comprehensive knowledge and practical skills. With the flexibility to learn at one's own pace and access to course materials anytime, online courses are a great way to stay educated and up-to-date.

Follow experts and thought leaders on social media: Social media has become a powerful tool for staying informed and connected. Following experts and thought leaders on social media platforms like Twitter, LinkedIn, and Facebook can provide valuable insights and keep one updated on industry trends and developments. It also allows for interaction and discussion, making it easier to clarify doubts and engage in meaningful conversations.

Listen to podcasts: Podcasts have gained popularity in recent years as an effective medium for learning and staying up-to-date. With a wide range of topics and hosts, one can find podcasts on almost any subject of interest. They offer convenient and flexible learning opportunities, as they can be listened to while commuting, exercising, or doing household chores. Many podcasts feature interviews with experts, providing valuable insights and knowledge.

Subscribe to newsletters and magazines: Another way to stay educated and up-to-date is by subscribing to newsletters and magazines. Many publications offer email newsletters that provide regular updates on relevant topics and news. Subscribing to magazines within one's field of interest can also provide in-depth articles, research, and insights on current affairs and trends. These resources can be conveniently accessed digitally and provide a great way to stay informed.

Engage in discussions and debates: Engaging in discussions and debates with others who share similar interests can provide a great learning opportunity. It allows for the exchange of ideas, perspectives, and information on a subject. Online forums, interest-based groups, and social media communities are a few platforms where one can engage in such discussions and debates.

Staying educated and up-to-date is crucial for personal and professional growth. With advancements in technology and access to information, there are various ways to stay informed and knowledgeable. It is essential to utilize a combination of these methods to expand one's knowledge, gain new skills, and stay updated on current trends and developments in today's ever-changing world.

Chapter 2
Goal Setting

Goal setting is the process of identifying, defining, and setting targets or objectives one wishes to achieve in the future. It is a tool used in personal and professional development to help individuals clarify their priorities, focus their efforts and utilize their time and resources effectively.

The process of goal setting involves reflecting on one's values, interests, strengths, and weaknesses to determine what is important and what one wants to achieve. Then, specific and measurable goals are created, along with a timeline for achieving them. These goals should be realistic and achievable, yet challenging enough to motivate and push individuals to work towards them.

The advantages of goal setting include increased motivation, focus, and direction in life. It helps individuals to stay organized and on track towards achieving their desired outcomes, whether it be personal, career-related, or educational. It also provides a sense of fulfillment and satisfaction upon accomplishment and helps individuals understand the steps required to reach their goal.

To effectively set and achieve goals, it is important to follow the SMART criteria, which stands for Specific, Measurable, Achievable, Relevant, and Time-bound. This means that goals should be clearly defined, have a measurable outcome, be realistically attainable, align with one's values and aspirations, and have a set deadline.

Additionally, it is crucial to regularly review and adjust goals as needed. This allows individuals to track their progress, make necessary changes, and continue working towards their goals. It is also helpful to break down larger goals into smaller, manageable tasks, and to celebrate each milestone achieved along the way.

In summary, goal setting is a powerful tool for personal and professional growth. By defining and pursuing specific targets, individuals can increase their focus, motivation, and productivity, and ultimately create a more fulfilling and purposeful life.

Setting realistic and measurable goals

Setting realistic and measurable goals is an essential aspect of achieving success in any aspect of life. Whether it's personal or professional, setting goals helps us to focus our energy, time and resources in a strategic and efficient manner. However, it is important to understand that not all goals are created equal. Some goals may be unrealistic and unachievable, while others may not be measurable, making it difficult to track progress and determine whether they have been achieved or not. In this sense, it is crucial to have a systematic approach to setting goals that are both realistic and measurable.

First and foremost, it is important to set realistic goals. This means that the goals should be achievable and within your reach. Unrealistic goals are often demotivating and may lead to a sense of failure or disappointment when they are not met. To set realistic goals, take a step back and assess your current capabilities, resources, and time. Consider your strengths and weaknesses, as well as any external factors that may affect your ability to achieve the goal. Set a goal that is challenging yet attainable, and take into account any potential obstacles that may arise along the way.

In addition to being realistic, goals should also be measurable. This means that they should have a specific and quantifiable outcome. A measurable goal has clear criteria for success, making it easier to track progress and determine whether the goal has been achieved or not. To make a goal measurable, it is important to define it in specific terms. For example, instead of setting a vague goal of "saving money," a measurable goal would be "saving $500 by the end of the month." This makes it easier to track progress and make adjustments if necessary.

Furthermore, it is important to set a timeline for achieving the goal. This not only provides a sense of urgency, but it also helps to break down the goal into smaller, more manageable tasks. Without a timeframe, there is no sense of direction or motivation, and the goal may become overwhelming or forgotten altogether. Consider the resources and time available to you, and set a realistic timeline for achieving the goal.

Another important aspect of setting realistic and measurable goals is to make them relevant to your overall objectives. Goals should be aligned with your long-term values and aspirations, and should contribute to your personal or professional growth. This ensures that you are motivated and committed to achieving the goal, as it has significance and relevance to your life.

Lastly, it is crucial to regularly review and assess your progress towards the goal. This not only helps to track progress, but it also allows for adjustments and modifications if necessary. If you find that you are not making sufficient progress towards the goal, reassess and make necessary changes to your approach. On the other hand, if you have achieved the goal, take time to celebrate your success and set new goals to continue your growth and development.

In conclusion, setting realistic and measurable goals is essential for achieving success in any aspect of life. By setting goals that are achievable, specific, and relevant, with a realistic timeline and constant evaluation, you can effectively work towards your objectives and celebrate your achievements. Remember to stay motivated, persistent, and open to adjusting your approach as needed. With a clear vision and strategic goal setting, success is within reach.

Importance of setting attainable goals

Setting attainable goals is crucial for personal and professional growth. It gives direction to our actions, motivates us to work towards something meaningful, and helps us stay focused on achieving our objectives. Without attainable goals, we may wander aimlessly, waste time and resources, and eventually feel overwhelmed and defeated. Therefore, it is essential to understand the importance of setting attainable goals and how it can benefit us in the long run.

Provides Clarity and Direction: Setting attainable goals gives us a clear understanding of what we want to achieve and how we want to achieve it. It helps us break down our larger goals into smaller, achievable tasks, making our path towards success more manageable and less intimidating. This clarity and direction set the foundation for effective decision-making, ensuring that we stay on track and make progress towards our goals.

Motivates and Increases Productivity: Goals give us a sense of purpose and motivate us to put in our best efforts to accomplish them. When our goals are attainable, we are more likely to stay committed and motivated to achieve them.

This, in turn, increases our productivity as we are focused on our goals and willing to put in the necessary time and effort to accomplish them.

Encourages Personal Growth: Goals that are attainable push us out of our comfort zone and challenge us to become better versions of ourselves. As we strive to reach our goals, we are forced to learn new skills, acquire new knowledge, and adopt new habits. This process of growth not only helps us achieve our goals but also develops our potential and enhances our capabilities in the long run.

Measures Progress and Success: Setting attainable goals provides us with a benchmark to measure our progress and helps us stay accountable. It gives us a sense of achievement every time we make progress towards our goals or accomplish them. This feeling of success not only boosts our confidence but also encourages us to set new, challenging goals for ourselves.

Helps in Time Management and Prioritization: When we have a clear set of attainable goals, we can prioritize our tasks and manage our time effectively. We can focus on the most important tasks that align with our goals and avoid getting distracted by less relevant activities. This allows us to make the most of our time and resources, making us more efficient in achieving our goals.

Reduces Stress and Increases Well-Being: Setting unattainable goals can lead to stress, anxiety, and disappointment. On the other hand, setting attainable goals and achieving them can boost our overall well-being and reduce stress levels. When we set realistic goals, we are more likely to have a positive outlook, be satisfied with our progress, and have a healthier work-life balance.

Setting attainable goals is crucial for our personal and professional growth. It not only gives us direction and clarity but also motivates us, encourages our personal growth, measures our progress, helps in time management, and reduces stress. By setting attainable goals, we can achieve success and lead a fulfilling life.

Methods for setting achievable goals

Setting achievable goals is an essential step in achieving success in any aspect of life. Whether it is in our personal or professional lives, having clear and achievable goals helps us stay focused and motivated, leading us towards the path of success. However, setting achievable goals can be a tricky task, and many people struggle to do it effectively. In this article, we will discuss some methods that can help you set achievable goals.

Identify your purpose and vision: The first step in setting achievable goals is to identify your purpose and vision. This means understanding why you want to achieve a particular goal and how it aligns with your long-term vision. Identifying your purpose will help you stay motivated and focused, even when faced with challenges along the way.

Use the SMART method: The SMART method is a goal-setting technique that stands for Specific, Measurable, Achievable, Relevant, and Time-bound. When setting achievable goals, it is essential to make sure they are specific, measurable, and have a deadline. This method helps you break down your goals into smaller, achievable targets, making it easier to track your progress.

Prioritize your goals: It is important to prioritize your goals based on their importance and urgency. This will help you focus on the most crucial goals first and avoid feeling overwhelmed by having too many goals at once. Prioritizing your goals will also help you stay on track and avoid wasting time and effort on goals that are less important.

Set realistic expectations: It is crucial to set realistic expectations when setting achievable goals. This means being honest with yourself about your capabilities and limitations. Setting goals that are too ambitious or unrealistic can lead to disappointment and demotivation. It is important to challenge yourself, but also be realistic about what you can achieve.

Break down your goals into smaller tasks: Breaking down your goals into smaller, manageable tasks can make them seem less daunting and more achievable. This also allows you to track your progress and make any necessary adjustments along the way. It is important to set achievable deadlines for each task to keep yourself motivated and on track.

Develop an action plan: Having a clear action plan is crucial for achieving any goal. It helps you stay organized, motivated and provides a roadmap for achieving your goals. Your action plan should include specific steps and deadlines for each task, as well as potential obstacles and how you will overcome them.

Stay accountable: One of the best ways to ensure you stay on track and achieve your goals is to be accountable. This could mean sharing your goals with a friend, a mentor, or joining a goal-setting group. Being accountable to someone else can provide you with the necessary support and motivation, and make it harder for you to give up on your goals.

Setting achievable goals requires a combination of clarity, planning, and determination. By following these methods and continuously evaluating and adjusting your goals, you can set yourself up for success. Remember to celebrate your accomplishments along the way, as this will help you stay motivated and inspired on your journey towards achieving your goals.

Breaking down long-term goals into smaller milestones

Long-term goals are those ambitious targets that we set for ourselves to achieve in the future. These goals often take months or even years to accomplish, making them seem overwhelming and difficult to attain. This is why it is essential to break down long-term goals into smaller milestones or short-term goals. Doing so not only makes these goals more manageable and achievable but also helps to stay motivated and focused.

Here are some steps that can help in breaking down long-term goals into smaller milestones:

Identify the long-term goal: The first step in this process is to clearly identify and establish the long-term goal. For example, a long-term goal could be to start a successful business or to lose 50 pounds in a year.

Set a timeline: Once the long-term goal is identified, it is crucial to set a realistic timeline for achieving it. This timeline will serve as a guide and can be adjusted as needed.

Divide the timeline into smaller chunks: Now that you have a timeline, the next step is to divide it into smaller chunks or milestones. These milestones should be realistic and achievable within a shorter time frame. For example, if the long-term goal is to lose 50 pounds in a year, the milestones could be to lose 5 pounds every month.

Create a plan: Once you have identified the milestones, it is essential to create a detailed plan that outlines the specific tasks that need to be done to achieve each milestone. This plan should include a step-by-step approach to help you stay on track and make progress.

Track your progress: As you start working towards your milestones, it is crucial to track your progress. This will help you to stay motivated and make any necessary adjustments to your plan if needed. Tracking your progress also allows you to celebrate the small victories and keep the momentum going.

Stay focused and motivated: Breaking down long-term goals into smaller milestones makes them more achievable, but it still requires discipline and determination to stay on track. It is essential to stay focused on the end goal and keep yourself motivated by reminding yourself of the progress you have made so far.

Re-evaluate and adjust: It is normal for circumstances or priorities to change while working towards long-term goals. Therefore, it is crucial to periodically re-evaluate your plan and make adjustments as needed. This will help to keep you on track and ensure that you are still working towards the overall long-term goal.

Breaking down long-term goals into smaller milestones not only makes them more achievable but also provides a roadmap for reaching the end goal. It helps to prevent overwhelm and allows for more flexibility in achieving the long-term goal. Moreover, by celebrating the small victories along the way, it can provide a sense of accomplishment and keep you motivated to keep pushing towards the ultimate goal.

Breaking down long-term goals into smaller milestones is a crucial step in achieving success. It allows you to focus on smaller, achievable tasks, which will ultimately lead to reaching the long-term goal. By setting a realistic timeline, creating a plan, tracking progress, and staying motivated, you can break down even the most challenging long-term goals into achievable milestones. So, if you have a long-term goal in mind, don't be afraid to break it down and start working towards your milestones today.

Benefits of breaking down goals

Goals serve as important guiding principles in one's personal and professional life. They provide a sense of direction, purpose, and motivation to achieve something specific. However, sometimes we may have lofty, unrealistic, or overwhelming goals that seem too big to tackle all at once. This is where breaking down goals can be beneficial. Breaking down goals is the process of dividing a complex or large goal into smaller and more manageable tasks that can be achieved in shorter time periods. This approach has numerous benefits that can greatly enhance our chances of achieving our goals. Let us take a look at them in detail:

Increases Clarity: When we break down a larger goal into smaller tasks, it becomes clearer and easier to understand. This is because each task has a specific purpose and contributes to the overall goal, making it easier to focus on what needs to be done. This clarity helps us stay on track and avoid feeling overwhelmed.

Enhances Time Management: Breaking down goals allows us to create a timeline and set a deadline for each task. This helps us manage our time more effectively and ensures that we are making progress towards our goal. It also enables us to prioritize our tasks and focus on the ones that are most important or urgent.

Boosts Motivation: Having a large goal can be intimidating and often leads to procrastination. Breaking it down into smaller tasks makes it feel more achievable and less daunting. This, in turn, boosts our motivation as we can now see the progress we are making and feel a sense of accomplishment after completing each task.

Promotes Focus: Multiple tasks and a large goal can make it difficult to focus on one thing at a time. By breaking down goals, we are able to focus on one task at a time, without being distracted by the bigger picture. This allows us to give our full attention and energy to each task, leading to better quality work and increased productivity.

Facilitates Checkpoints: Breaking down goals into smaller tasks allows us to create milestones or checkpoints along the way. These checkpoints act as a way to measure our progress and determine if we are on track to achieving our goal. If we are falling behind, we can make necessary adjustments to our plan to get back on track.

Increases Flexibility: Sometimes, unexpected situations may arise that prevent us from achieving our goals within the set timeline. When we have broken down our goals, it becomes easier to adjust and adapt our plan to accommodate these changes. This flexibility helps us stay on track and continue making progress towards our goal.

Helps in Problem-Solving: By breaking down goals, we can identify potential roadblocks and challenges that may come up during the process. This allows us to anticipate and plan for these obstacles, making it easier to overcome them when they do arise. It also gives us the chance to come up with alternative solutions and strategies if needed.

Consequently, breaking down goals into smaller, more manageable tasks can greatly enhance our chances of achieving them. It helps us stay organized, focused, and motivated, while also allowing flexibility and adaptability. By following this approach, we can make our goals seem more attainable, and the step-by-step progress we make towards them can give us a sense of accomplishment and satisfaction.

Tips for setting achievable milestones

Milestones are a set of specific and measurable goals that are used to track progress towards a larger goal or objective. Whether you are working towards personal, academic, or professional goals, setting achievable milestones is crucial for success. These milestones serve as checkpoints that help you stay on track, monitor your progress, and make adjustments if necessary. Here are some tips for setting achievable milestones:

Define your end goal clearly: The first step to setting achievable milestones is to have a clear understanding of your ultimate goal. What do you want to achieve? What is the purpose of your goal? Having a clear and specific end goal will help you set realistic milestones that align with your overall objective.

Break down your goal into smaller tasks: Once you have a clear understanding of your end goal, break it down into smaller, more manageable tasks. This will make the goal less overwhelming and help you focus on one step at a time. Each task can then be turned into a milestone, making it easier to track your progress.

Make your milestones specific and measurable: The key to setting achievable milestones is to make them specific and measurable. This means defining exactly what needs to be accomplished and setting a deadline for each milestone. For example, instead of setting a milestone of "improve my writing skills," make it more specific and measurable by setting a milestone of "write one blog post per week for the next three months."

Be realistic: It is important to be realistic when setting milestones. This means acknowledging your current abilities, resources, and limitations. Setting unrealistic milestones will only lead to frustration and demotivation when they are not achieved. Consider your daily schedule, workload, and other commitments before setting your milestones.

Use the SMART criteria: The SMART criteria is a useful tool for setting achievable milestones. This stands for Specific,

Measurable, Attainable, Relevant, and Time-bound. Your milestones should meet all of these criteria to ensure that they are realistic and achievable. For example, your milestone of "lose 20 pounds in one month" may not be attainable or healthy, but "lose 10 pounds in two months" may be more achievable.

Prioritize your milestones: Not all milestones are equal, some may be more critical for achieving your ultimate goal than others. Therefore, it is essential to prioritize your milestones. This will help you focus your time and energy on the most important tasks, making it easier to achieve your overall goal.

Celebrate your achievements: Celebrating your achievements, no matter how small they may seem, is crucial for staying motivated and on track. This doesn't mean throwing a big party every time you reach a milestone, but rather acknowledging your progress and giving yourself a pat on the back. This will help you maintain a positive mindset and keep you inspired to reach the next milestone.

Review and adjust as needed: Setting achievable milestones does not mean that they cannot be adjusted along the way. It is essential to regularly review your progress and make adjustments if necessary. If you find that a milestone is too easy or too challenging, make the necessary changes to keep yourself on track.

Setting achievable milestones is vital for success in reaching your goals. With these tips in mind, you can break down your larger goals into smaller, more manageable tasks that make the overall goal seem less daunting. Remember to be realistic, use the SMART criteria, prioritize your milestones, and celebrate your achievements along the way. By doing so, you will be able to stay motivated and on track towards reaching your ultimate goal.

Creating a plan of action

Creating a plan of action is an essential component of achieving any goal or completing a task efficiently and effectively. It is a strategic approach towards accomplishing desired outcomes by outlining all the necessary steps and resources needed to achieve a specific objective. A well-constructed plan of action provides a roadmap for success, helping individuals or teams to stay focused, organized, and on track towards their goals.

The process of creating a plan of action involves several key steps that need to be carefully considered and followed to ensure its effectiveness. These steps may include identifying the objective, understanding the current situation, setting realistic goals and deadlines, determining the necessary resources, and creating a timeline for implementation.

The first step in creating a plan of action is to clearly define the objective. This involves understanding the purpose of the plan and what the desired outcome is. It is crucial to have a clear and specific objective to give direction and focus to the overall plan.

The next step is to assess the current situation. This involves evaluating the current resources, capabilities, and any potential challenges or obstacles that may hinder the achievement of the objective. Understanding the current state of affairs is crucial in creating a realistic and effective plan of action.

Once the objective and current situation have been determined, the next step is to set realistic goals and deadlines. These goals and deadlines should be specific, measurable, achievable, relevant, and time-bound (SMART). This allows for better tracking and monitoring of progress towards the overall objective.

After setting goals and deadlines, it is important to determine the necessary resources needed to achieve the objective. This can include human resources, financial resources, equipment, and any other relevant resources. It is essential to ensure that all necessary resources are readily available to avoid any delays in the implementation of the plan.

Creating a timeline for implementation is the next critical step in creating a plan of action. This involves breaking down the plan into smaller, actionable tasks and assigning specific deadlines for each task. This allows for better management and monitoring of progress towards achieving the overall objective.

Once the plan of action has been developed, it is essential to communicate it to all individuals or teams involved. This helps to ensure that everyone is on the same page and understands their roles and responsibilities in the implementation of the plan.

Finally, regular monitoring and evaluation of the plan are crucial for its success. This allows for any necessary adjustments to be made in order to keep the plan on track and ensure that the desired outcomes are being achieved.

Creating a plan of action is a crucial step towards accomplishing any goal or completing a task successfully. By following the steps outlined above, individuals or teams can create a well-structured and organized plan of action that will help guide them towards achieving their objectives in an efficient and effective manner. A well-constructed plan of action not only increases the chances of success but also helps to reduce stress and confusion, leading to a more positive and productive working environment.

Steps for creating an effective plan of action

Creating a plan of action is essential in achieving success, whether it be in personal or professional endeavors. It serves as a roadmap that outlines the steps and strategies needed to reach a specific goal or solve a problem. An effective plan of action is crucial in ensuring that resources are utilized efficiently and that the desired outcome is achieved.

Define the goal or objective
The first step in creating an effective plan of action is to clearly define the goal or

objective. This should be specific, measurable, achievable, relevant, and time-bound (SMART). It serves as a foundation for the entire plan and helps to provide focus and direction.

Conduct a thorough assessment

Before creating a plan of action, it is important to assess the current situation, resources, and any potential obstacles. This may involve analyzing data, conducting research, or seeking input from team members or relevant stakeholders. This will help to identify any gaps or areas that need improvement to achieve the desired goal.

Set priorities and establish timelines

Based on the assessment, prioritize the tasks or actions that are necessary to achieve the goal. This will help to determine the order in which tasks should be completed and the estimated timeline for each task. It is essential to set realistic and achievable timelines to avoid unnecessary stress or delays.

Determine the necessary resources

To effectively execute the plan, it is important to identify and allocate the necessary resources. This may include budget, personnel, materials, equipment, or other support services. Ensuring that all necessary resources are available is crucial in the successful implementation of the plan.

Identify potential challenges and risks

Anticipating potential challenges and risks can help to prevent or minimize their impact on the plan. It is important to identify and analyze any potential obstacles or risks that may arise, and develop contingency plans to address them.

Develop a detailed action plan

Based on all the information gathered, develop a detailed action plan that outlines the specific steps and strategies needed to achieve the desired goal. This should include the tasks, responsible individuals or teams, deadlines, and expected outcomes for each action.

Communicate and collaborate

Effective communication and collaboration are crucial in implementing an action plan successfully. Ensure that all team members are aware of their roles and responsibilities, and regularly communicate progress, challenges, and changes in the plan. This will help to keep everyone on track and make necessary adjustments if needed.

Monitor and evaluate progress

Regularly monitoring and evaluating the progress of the plan is important to ensure that it is on track and achieving the desired results. This will help to identify any areas that may require adjustments or improvements.

Make necessary adjustments

Based on the monitoring and evaluation, make necessary adjustments to the plan as needed. When faced with unexpected obstacles or changes, be flexible and adapt the plan accordingly to ensure its effectiveness.

Celebrate successes and learn from failures

As the plan is executed, it is important to celebrate successes and acknowledge the efforts of the team. This will help to boost morale and motivate team members to continue working towards the goal. However, if there are any failures or setbacks, it is important to learn from them and make necessary improvements for future plans.

In conclusion, creating an effective plan of action requires careful planning, communication, and collaboration. By following these steps, you can develop a well-structured plan that will help you achieve your goals and objectives efficiently and effectively. Remember to regularly review and make necessary adjustments as the plan progresses to ensure its success.

Importance of having a plan

Having a plan is crucial for achieving success and reaching our goals in life. It helps us to have a clear direction and focus, and steer our actions towards the desired outcome. Whether it is in our personal lives or professional endeavors, having a plan can make all the difference between success and failure. In this essay, we will discuss the importance of having a plan and how it can benefit us in various aspects of our lives.

Provides clarity and purpose:
Having a plan helps us to define our goals and objectives clearly. It outlines what we want to achieve, why it is important to us, and how we can attain it. This provides a sense of direction and purpose, which can help us stay motivated and focused, even when faced with challenges and obstacles.

Helps in effective time management:
Time is a precious resource, and having a plan allows us to make the most of it. With a plan in place, we can prioritize our tasks, set deadlines, and allocate our time efficiently to accomplish our goals. This ensures that we do not waste time on unimportant or trivial tasks, and instead focus on what is essential.

Increases productivity:
A well-defined plan helps us to be more organized and structured in our approach, which leads to increased productivity. When

we have a clear roadmap of what needs to be done, it becomes easier to break down tasks into smaller and manageable chunks. This helps us to stay on track and complete our tasks efficiently, thus increasing our productivity.

Reduces stress:
Having a plan can reduce stress and anxiety levels significantly. It gives us a sense of control and eliminates the fear of the unknown, which can often lead to stress and worry. With a plan in place, we know exactly what we need to do and how to go about it, which can help us feel more confident and in control.

Allows for effective resource management:
A plan helps us to identify the resources we need to achieve our goals and manage them efficiently. Whether it is financial, human, or material resources, having a plan allows us to allocate them appropriately and make the best use of them. This ensures that we do not waste our resources and optimize them to achieve the desired results.

Facilitates decision-making:
Having a plan helps us to make informed decisions that align with our goals and objectives. It acts as a reference point and provides us with a framework to evaluate our options and make the best decisions. This helps us to avoid impulsive or irrational decisions that may hinder our progress towards our goals.

Encourages adaptability and flexibility:
While having a plan is essential, it is also important to be adaptable and flexible when necessary. Having a plan allows us to identify potential roadblocks and prepare for them, but it also allows us to modify our approach if needed. This allows us to be more resilient and adjust to unexpected situations without compromising on our goals.

Having a plan is crucial for success and achieving our goals. It provides us with clarity, purpose, and direction, and helps us to manage our time and resources effectively. It also reduces stress, facilitates decision-making, and encourages adaptability. Therefore, it is essential to have a plan in place to maximize our chances of success in all aspects of our lives.

Chapter 3
Time Management

Prioritizing tasks

Time management is the process of organizing and planning how to allocate your time effectively and efficiently to make the most out of every day. It is a crucial skill to develop, not only in a professional setting but also in personal life. Managing time effectively enables individuals to achieve their goals, reduce stress, and improve productivity. It is one of the most critical aspects of success, as how well you manage your time can determine your overall success and satisfaction in life.

A key element of time management is prioritizing tasks. Prioritization involves identifying the tasks that need to be completed first and organizing them in order of importance. This helps individuals to focus on the tasks that are most urgent and critical, ensuring that they are completed on time.

One effective way to prioritize tasks is using the Eisenhower Matrix. It is a simple four-quadrant grid that helps individuals to categorize tasks based on their level of urgency and importance. The top-left quadrant consists of tasks that are both urgent and important, and these should be given the highest priority. These are often tasks with set deadlines, such as work projects or school assignments that cannot be delayed. The top-right quadrant consists of tasks that are important but not necessarily urgent, such as long-term projects or personal development activities. These should be scheduled and given attention after completing the urgent tasks. The bottom-left quadrant represents tasks that are urgent but not important, such as answering emails or attending meetings. These can often be delegated or minimized to free up time for more significant tasks. The bottom-right quadrant consists of tasks that are neither urgent nor important and should be avoided or reduced as they tend to waste time.

Another useful method for prioritizing tasks is the ABCDE method, where tasks are categorized into five levels: A for urgent and critical, B for important, C for tasks that can be delegated, D for tasks that can be delayed, and E for tasks that can be eliminated. By categorizing tasks in this way, individuals can ensure that the most critical tasks are completed first, followed by others in order of importance.

Effective time management also involves setting clear and achievable goals and deadlines for each task. This not only helps individuals to stay focused but also provides a sense of direction and motivation. Breaking down large tasks into smaller, manageable chunks can also be useful in managing time and reducing feelings of overwhelm.

Another important aspect of prioritizing tasks is learning to say no. Often, individuals may feel pressured to take on additional tasks and responsibilities, even if they do not have the time. It is essential to evaluate whether these tasks align with one's goals and priorities and assess if taking them on will lead to burnout or lack of focus on more crucial tasks.

In addition to prioritizing tasks, effective time management also involves creating a schedule or to-do list. This helps individuals to plan their day and allocate time for each task. It is essential to be realistic and leave enough time for breaks and unexpected interruptions. It is also crucial to schedule tasks during times when one is most productive and focused.

To manage time effectively, individuals must also learn to overcome procrastination. Procrastination can lead to delays in completing tasks and increase stress levels. It is crucial to identify the root cause of procrastination and find ways to overcome it, such as breaking down tasks into smaller, more manageable chunks or setting strict deadlines for oneself.

Time management is a critical skill that everyone should strive to develop.

Prioritizing tasks is a key aspect of time management, and individuals must learn to categorize tasks based on urgency and importance. By setting clear goals, creating a schedule, and avoiding procrastination, individuals can effectively manage their time and achieve their desired outcomes. It takes practice and discipline to master time management, but the benefits of increased productivity, reduced stress, and overall satisfaction make it worth the effort.

Importance of prioritizing

Prioritizing is the act of arranging tasks, activities, or goals in order of importance. It involves making deliberate and conscious decisions about where to allocate time, energy, and resources. Prioritization is a crucial skill that plays a significant role in various aspects of our lives, including personal, professional, and academic. It helps individuals and organizations to focus on what truly matters, increase productivity, and achieve desired results. In this essay, we will discuss the importance of prioritizing and how it can benefit individuals and organizations.

Firstly, prioritizing allows individuals to manage their time effectively. Time is a limited resource, and we all have 24 hours in a day. However, how we use our time determines our productivity and success. By prioritizing, individuals can identify the most critical tasks or goals and allocate time accordingly. This helps to avoid wasting time on less important activities and focus on what will bring the most significant impact. As a result, individuals can accomplish more within a given time.

Moreover, prioritizing assists in reducing stress and increasing efficiency. When we have too many things on our to-do list, it can be overwhelming and stressful, leading to burnout. However, by prioritizing, we can break down tasks into manageable chunks and work through them systematically. This not only reduces stress but also increases efficiency as it helps individuals to concentrate on one task at a time and complete it before moving on to the next.

Prioritizing also allows individuals to set and achieve goals effectively. Often, we have numerous goals, both short-term and long-term. Prioritizing helps individuals to determine which goals are most important and require immediate attention. By focusing on these priorities, goals can be achieved more efficiently and effectively. This is especially crucial for organizations, where there are multiple projects and objectives. Prioritizing enables organizations to set achievable goals, allocate appropriate resources, and monitor progress, leading to success.

Another essential aspect of prioritizing is that it helps individuals and organizations to make better decisions. When faced with multiple options and tasks, it can be challenging to determine which one to focus on or which one will have the most significant impact. However, by prioritizing, individuals and organizations can evaluate the pros and cons of each option and choose the one that aligns with their priorities and goals. This helps to avoid wasting time and resources on less important tasks or choices.

Furthermore, prioritizing allows individuals to maintain a healthy work-life balance. Often, individuals can get caught up in work and neglect other important aspects of their lives, such as family, friends, and personal care. Prioritizing helps individuals to identify tasks that require immediate attention and those that can be postponed. This enables individuals to create a balance between work and personal life, which is essential for overall well-being and happiness.

Finally, prioritizing promotes efficiency and effectiveness in organizations. In today's fast-paced business world, organizations have to deal with multiple tasks, projects, and goals simultaneously. This can be overwhelming and can lead to chaos and. However, by prioritizing, organizations can focus on crucial tasks and allocate resources and manpower accordingly. This leads to efficient and effective use of resources, increased productivity, and improved overall performance.

Therefore, prioritizing is essential for individuals and organizations seeking to achieve success and maintain a healthy work-life balance. It allows individuals to manage time effectively, reduce stress, set and achieve goals, make better decisions, and maintain a healthy work-life balance. In organizations, prioritizing promotes efficiency and effectiveness, leading to improved performance. Therefore, mastering the skill of prioritizing is crucial for personal and professional growth and success.

Strategies for effective prioritization

Prioritization is a crucial aspect of productivity and time management. It involves identifying and organizing tasks or activities in order of importance, urgency, or relevance. Effective prioritization ensures that you focus your time, energy, and resources on the most critical tasks, thereby increasing efficiency and productivity. However, prioritization is not always an easy task, and it requires a strategic approach to be effective. In this article, we will discuss strategies for effective prioritization.

Identify Your Goals and Objectives
The first step to effective prioritization is to define your goals and objectives. This will provide a clear understanding of what you aim to achieve and what tasks or activities are essential to meet those goals. Ask yourself what your priorities are, both short-term and long-term, and use them as a guide to prioritize your tasks.

Use the Eisenhower Matrix
The Eisenhower Matrix, also known as the Urgent-Important Matrix, is a popular time management tool that can help you prioritize tasks effectively. It divides tasks into four quadrants based on their urgency and importance, helping you identify which tasks are essential and which ones can be delegated, postponed, or eliminated. This method allows you to focus your time and efforts on tasks that align with your goals and have the most significant impact.

Assess Time and Resource Constraints

Prioritizing effectively also involves considering the time and resources available for each task. Some tasks may have strict deadlines, while others may be more flexible. Similarly, some tasks may require more resources, such as money or people, to complete. By assessing these constraints, you can determine which tasks need to be prioritized to ensure they are completed on time and within the available resources.

Consider the Consequences

When prioritizing tasks, it is essential to consider the consequences of not completing them. Some tasks may have severe consequences if not completed, while others may not have a significant impact. By evaluating the potential consequences, you can give priority to tasks that can positively or negatively affect your goals and objectives.

Focus on One Task at a Time

Trying to juggle multiple tasks at once can be overwhelming and reduce your productivity. It is essential to focus on one task at a time to complete it efficiently. Once you have prioritized your tasks, assign a specific time to work on each one and avoid multitasking. This will prevent you from getting sidetracked and help you complete tasks more effectively.

Learn to Say No
One of the biggest challenges of prioritization is the constant influx of new tasks or requests that disrupt your schedule. As much as possible, learn to say no to tasks that do not align with your goals or are not a priority at the moment. This will help you maintain focus on your priorities and avoid taking on more than you can handle.

Review and Adjust Priorities Regularly
Priorities can change as circumstances and goals change. It is essential to review and adjust priorities regularly to ensure you are working on the most important tasks. You may need to reprioritize tasks based on their urgency, importance, or new information. This practice will help you stay on top of your goals and ensure that your efforts are directed towards tasks that matter the most.

In conclusion, effective prioritization is crucial for maximizing productivity and achieving your goals. By following these strategies, you can better manage your time, focus on essential tasks, and achieve your objectives efficiently. Prioritization is a skill that takes time and practice to master, but with these strategies, you can develop a prioritization system that works best for you.

Eliminating time-wasters

R&D (Research and Development) is a crucial aspect of any organization as it is the driving force behind innovation, growth, and competitive advantage. However, managing R&D funds can be a challenging task as it involves a high level of uncertainty and risk. One of the major challenges faced by R&D managers is the effective utilization of funds and the elimination of time-wasters.

Time-wasters can be defined as any activity or process that consumes time and resources without adding value to the R&D project. These time-wasters not only have a negative impact on the project timeline but also on the organization's overall profitability and competitiveness. Therefore, it is essential for R&D managers to identify and eliminate these time-wasters to ensure the efficient utilization of funds and resources.

Here are some ways to eliminate time-wasters from R&D funds management:

Clear allocation of roles and responsibilities: The first step in eliminating time-wasters is to have a clear understanding of roles and responsibilities within the R&D team. Each team member should have a defined scope of work and should be held accountable for their tasks. This will ensure that everyone is working towards a common goal and there is no duplication of work or time wasted on unnecessary tasks.

Risk assessment and management: Risk is an inherent part of R&D projects, and it is crucial to assess and manage it effectively. Conducting a risk assessment at the beginning of a project can help in identifying potential time-wasters and developing a plan to mitigate them. This will help R&D managers to proactively address any risks that may arise and prevent wasting time and resources on unforeseen issues.

Streamlining processes: R&D projects involve multiple processes, and inefficiencies in these processes can lead to time wastage. It is important to review and streamline these processes regularly to eliminate any unnecessary steps or activities. This will not only save time but also improve the overall efficiency of the project.

Regular monitoring and evaluation: Monitoring and evaluation are essential for effective R&D funds management. Regularly tracking project progress, budget, and resource allocation can help identify any deviations or delays. This will enable R&D managers to take corrective actions and prevent any wastage of time and resources.

Effective communication: Poor communication can lead to misunderstandings, delays, and rework, all of which can be major time-wasters. Establishing open and effective communication channels within the R&D team and with external stakeholders is crucial. This will ensure that everyone is on the same page, and any issues or concerns are addressed in a timely manner.

Prioritization of projects: In many organizations, R&D teams are working on multiple projects simultaneously. This can lead to a lack of focus and delayed timelines if not managed effectively. It is essential to prioritize projects based on their strategic importance and allocate resources accordingly. This will help in avoiding time-wasters and ensuring that critical projects are completed on time.

Use of technology: Technology has revolutionized the way R&D projects are managed. It has made communication, collaboration, and project tracking much more efficient. R&D managers should leverage technology to streamline processes, improve communication, and make data-driven decisions. This will help in identifying and eliminating time-wasters more effectively.

Eliminating time-wasters from R&D funds management requires a proactive approach and constant monitoring. By following the above-mentioned strategies, R&D managers can minimize wastage of time and resources, and ensure the successful completion of projects within the allocated budget and timeline. This, in turn, will lead to increased efficiency and competitiveness for the organization.

Identifying time-wasters

As said earlier, Time-wasters are activities or behaviors that consume a significant amount of time without producing any desired results or outcomes. These can range from minor distractions to major disruptions in our daily lives. Time-wasters can significantly affect our productivity, leaving us feeling overwhelmed, stressed, and unproductive. Therefore, identifying time-wasters is crucial as it enables us to eliminate or minimize their impact on our daily routines.

Here are some common time-wasters and strategies to identify them:

Social media and internet browsing: With the widespread use of social media platforms and the ease of internet access, many people find themselves wasting hours scrolling through news feeds, watching videos, or browsing aimlessly. This is a significant time-waster that can greatly affect our productivity. To identify this time-waster, track your internet usage using apps or the screen time feature on your phone. If you find yourself spending hours on social media or browsing the internet without any specific purpose, it might be a time-waster for you.

Meetings and discussions: Meetings and discussions can be necessary for work, but they can also turn into time-wasters if not managed effectively. If you find yourself attending meetings that do not have a clear objective or agenda, or if they go on longer than necessary, it can be a significant waste of time. To identify this, keep track of the meetings you attend, their duration, and whether the objectives were met. If you find yourself attending meetings that do not contribute to your work or goals, it might be a time-waster for you.

Procrastination: Procrastination is the act of delaying or avoiding important tasks and replacing them with less critical tasks. It is a common time-waster that can significantly affect our productivity. To identify procrastination, pay attention to when you delay or avoid important tasks and what you do in the meantime. If you find yourself engaging in less important tasks instead of the important ones, it might be a sign of procrastination.

Multitasking: Many people believe that multitasking is an efficient way to get more things done in less time. However, research shows that multitasking can decrease productivity as it divides our attention and makes it difficult to focus on one task at a time. To identify multitasking as a time-waster, pay attention to how often you switch back and forth between tasks and whether it affects the quality of your work. If you find yourself losing focus and making more mistakes while multitasking, it might be a time-waster for you.

Perfectionism: Striving for perfection is a commendable trait, but it can also become a time-waster when taken to the extreme. Trying to make everything perfect can consume a lot of time and may not be necessary for every task. To identify perfectionism as a time-waster, observe how long you spend on specific tasks and whether it affects your ability to complete other tasks. If you find yourself spending an excessive amount of time on tasks that do not require perfection, it might be a time-waster for you.

Email and notifications: Constant email checking and responding to notifications can disrupt our focus and consume a significant amount of time. To identify this as a time-waster, track the amount of time you spend on checking and responding to emails and notifications. If you find yourself spending more time than necessary on these activities, it might be a time-waster for you.

Being aware of our daily habits and routines can help us identify time-wasters. It is essential to note that what might be a time-waster for one person may not be for another. Therefore, it is crucial to identify and eliminate or minimize time-wasters based on our own individual habits and goals to improve productivity and overall well-being.

Tactics for eliminating time-wasters

Time management is a critical skill that everyone should possess, yet it is common for individuals to struggle with time-wasters in their daily lives. These are activities or tasks that consume a significant amount of time and add little or no value to our lives or productivity. Time-wasters can range from scrolling through social media for hours to constantly checking emails or attending unnecessary meetings. These seemingly small activities can quickly add up and consume a significant portion of our day, leaving us feeling unaccomplished and overwhelmed with unfinished tasks.

Eliminating time-wasters requires a deliberate and strategic approach. Here are some tactics that can help in eliminating time-wasters:

Identify and prioritize your tasks
The first step in eliminating time-wasters is to identify the tasks that are essential and those that are not. Make a to-do list and categorize the tasks into urgent, important, and non-essential. This will help you to focus on high-priority tasks, ensuring that they are completed within the allotted time.

Set realistic goals and deadlines
Setting realistic goals and deadlines can help you stay focused and motivated. Be specific about what you want to achieve and set a realistic timeline for each task. This will help you prioritize and eliminate any time-wasters that do not contribute to your goals.

Avoid procrastination

Procrastination is a major time-waster that often leads to a last-minute rush to complete tasks. Make a conscious effort to break the habit of procrastination by setting achievable goals and deadlines, and by taking breaks to avoid burnout. It's also helpful to identify the reasons behind your procrastination and find solutions to address them.

Limit distractions

In today's digital age, distractions are everywhere, and they can significantly impact our productivity. Identify and eliminate potential distractions such as social media, unnecessary notifications, or a noisy work environment. You can also use tools such as website blockers or time management apps to limit distractions and stay focused on the task at hand.

Delegate tasks

It's important to recognize that we cannot do everything by ourselves, and trying to do so can lead to time-wasting. Delegate tasks that can be completed by others, freeing up time for you to focus on more critical tasks.

Schedule breaks

Taking short breaks throughout the day can help improve productivity by providing time to recharge and refocus. Avoid continuously working without taking breaks as it can lead to burnout and decreased productivity.

Say "No"

It can be challenging to say no to requests for our time, but learning how to set boundaries is essential in eliminating time-wasters. If a task or meeting does not align with your priorities or goals, it's okay to decline or reschedule.

Generally, eliminating time-wasters requires discipline and a conscious effort to prioritize and manage your time effectively. By implementing these tactics, you can ultimately save time, increase productivity, and achieve your goals. Remember, time is a valuable resource, and it's up to us to use it wisely.

Productivity techniques

Productivity is defined as the ability to efficiently and effectively use resources to complete tasks and achieve goals. In today's fast-paced and highly competitive world, being productive is essential for success. But with endless distractions and constant demands on our time, it can be challenging to stay focused and accomplish our daily tasks. This is where productivity techniques come into play. They are methods or strategies that help individuals manage their time, prioritize tasks, and optimize their workflow to become more efficient and productive. In this essay, we will discuss some of the most effective productivity techniques that can help individuals increase their productivity.

Pomodoro technique

The Pomodoro technique is a time management method that was developed in the late 1980s by Francesco Cirillo. It is a simple yet effective technique that helps individuals manage their time and increase productivity by breaking their work into intervals, typically 25 minutes, followed by a short break. The technique is named after the tomato-shaped kitchen timer, also known as a "pomodoro," that Cirillo used to time his work intervals.

The basic concept of the Pomodoro technique is to divide work into shorter, focused segments, known as "pomodoros." Each pomodoro is a unit of time, usually 25 minutes, during which the individual focuses solely on the task at hand. After the completion of each pomodoro, a short 5-minute break is taken, and after four pomodoros, a more extended break of 15-30 minutes is taken. This cycle is repeated until the task is completed.

Implementing the Pomodoro technique can bring numerous benefits and improve productivity. The first advantage is that it encourages individuals to work with a sense of urgency and focus. The set time intervals and breaks create a sense of urgency, making it easier to start working and stay focused on the task. Additionally, by taking short breaks after each pomodoro, individuals can avoid burnout and maintain their energy levels throughout the day.

Moreover, the Pomodoro technique helps individuals overcome the procrastination trap. Many people struggle with starting a task or staying focused on it for an extended period. However, by breaking the work into smaller, manageable chunks, it becomes less daunting and more achievable. It also allows individuals to have a clear plan of what they need to accomplish during each pomodoro, making it easier to get started and stay on track.

The Pomodoro technique also promotes better time management. By breaking work into intervals, individuals can see how much time they spend on each task, allowing them to identify areas where they may be wasting time. This awareness enables them to become more efficient in managing their time and eliminate time-wasters, leading to increased productivity.

Another significant advantage of the Pomodoro technique is that it allows individuals to structure their day. By planning out tasks for each pomodoro, individuals can have a clear picture of what needs to be done, when it needs to be done, and how much time will be spent on it. This structure creates a sense of control and organization, reducing stress and providing a more balanced approach to work.

One of the key principles of the Pomodoro technique is the use of breaks. This technique recognizes that breaks are essential for maintaining productivity and creativity. By taking regular breaks, individuals can rest their brains, recharge their energy levels, and return to work with a fresh perspective. This promotes mental clarity and prevents burnout, allowing individuals to work more efficiently and effectively.

In addition to the benefits mentioned above, the Pomodoro technique also promotes a work-life balance. By taking regular breaks, individuals can step away from work and focus on other aspects of their life, such as family, friends, hobbies, and self-care. This balance is crucial for overall well-being and can lead to increased motivation and job satisfaction.

To implement the Pomodoro technique effectively, here are some tips:

Create a to-do list: Start by making a list of tasks that need to be accomplished in a day. Then prioritize them based on urgency and importance.

Set a timer: Use a timer or a Pomodoro app to set the 25-minute intervals, followed by breaks. This helps in staying on track and not getting carried away with distractions.

Take breaks: Make sure to take breaks at the end of each pomodoro. This time should be used for stepping away from work, stretching, walking, or any other relaxing activity.

Eliminate distractions: During the focused work periods, eliminate distractions by putting phones on silent, closing unnecessary tabs, or finding a quiet work environment.

Record progress: Keep track of the number of pomodoros completed and the tasks accomplished. This helps in identifying areas where more time is being spent and making adjustments accordingly.

The Pomodoro technique is a simple yet powerful tool for managing time, increasing productivity, and maintaining a work-life balance. By breaking work into manageable chunks and taking regular breaks, individuals can improve their focus, eliminate procrastination, and be more efficient in their work. Give it a try and see the positive impact it can make on your daily productivity.

Eisenhower matrix

The Eisenhower matrix, also known as the Eisenhower box or Eisenhower decision matrix, is a popular time management tool that was developed by former US President Dwight D. Eisenhower. Eisenhower used this method to prioritize tasks and make decisions while serving as the Supreme

Commander of the Allied Forces in World War II and later as the 34th President of the United States.

This matrix is used to categorize tasks based on their urgency and importance, in order to effectively manage time, increase productivity, and reduce stress. It consists of four quadrants that are divided by a vertical line and a horizontal line, creating a 2x2 grid.

The first quadrant, the "Important and Urgent" quadrant, is for tasks that are both important (i.e. have a significant impact on achieving one's goals) and urgent (i.e. require immediate attention). These tasks are top priorities and should be dealt with immediately to avoid negative consequences. Examples of tasks in this quadrant could be a work deadline, a medical emergency, or an urgent family matter.

The second quadrant, the "Important but Not Urgent" quadrant, is for tasks that are important but do not require immediate attention. These tasks are future-focused and require planning and proactive action. Neglecting these tasks can result in missed opportunities and goal failures. Examples of tasks in this quadrant could be personal development, strategic planning, or relationship building.

The third quadrant, the "Urgent but Not Important" quadrant, is for tasks that are urgent but do not contribute to long-term goals. These tasks are often time-consuming and can distract from important work. Examples of tasks in this quadrant could be responding to non-urgent emails or calls, attending to minor problems, or helping someone with a task that is not urgent or important.

The final quadrant, the "Not Important and Not Urgent" quadrant, is for tasks that are neither important nor urgent. These tasks provide little value and should be eliminated or delegated if possible. Examples of tasks in this quadrant could be scrolling through social media, watching TV, or indulging in other leisure activities.

Using the Eisenhower matrix, individuals can prioritize their tasks and make effective decisions by identifying which tasks are most important and require immediate attention. It also helps individuals to eliminate or delegate tasks that are not important or urgent, allowing them to focus on what truly matters.

One of the key benefits of using the Eisenhower matrix is that it helps individuals to be more productive and efficient with their time. By focusing on important tasks and eliminating or delegating less important ones, individuals can achieve more in less time. It also allows individuals to have a better work-life balance by ensuring that important personal and professional tasks are given equal priority.

Moreover, the Eisenhower matrix helps individuals avoid the trap of getting caught up in urgent tasks that may not contribute to their long-term goals. By taking a more proactive approach and focusing on important but non-urgent tasks, individuals can prevent future crises and accomplish their goals more effectively.

Generally, the Eisenhower matrix is a simple yet powerful tool for effective time management and decision-making. By categorizing tasks based on their urgency and importance, individuals can prioritize and manage their time efficiently, leading to increased productivity and reduced stress.

Other effective productivity techniques

The 80/20 Rule (or Pareto Principle): This principle states that 80% of results come from 20% of your efforts. By identifying and focusing on the most important and high-impact tasks, you can increase productivity and achieve more in a shorter time.

Task Batching: This technique involves grouping similar tasks together and completing them in batch mode, instead of doing them separately. This helps to minimize distractions and reduce the time and mental effort spent on switching between tasks.

Mind Mapping: This technique involves visually organizing ideas and information in a hierarchical or radial structure. It helps to stimulate creativity and improve memory retention, making it an effective tool for brainstorming and planning.

Time Blocking: This technique involves allocating specific time blocks for different tasks or activities. This not only helps to manage time efficiently but also encourages focused work and minimizes multitasking.

The ABCDE Method: This method, coined by Brian Tracy, involves assigning priorities to tasks by categorizing them as A (very important and requiring immediate action), B, C, D, and E (least important). This helps to focus on the most critical tasks and avoid wasting time on less important ones.

Kanban Method: This is a project management technique that involves using a visual board to track and manage tasks. Tasks are organized into different stages or columns, making it easier to track progress and prioritize tasks.

Eat the Frog Method: Coined by Mark Twain, this method suggests tackling the most challenging or unpleasant task first thing in the morning. This not only helps to get it out of the way but also sets the tone for a productive day.

Don't Break the Chain Method: This technique involves setting a daily goal and marking a cross or chain on a calendar for every day that the goal is achieved. The visual representation of progress serves as motivation to keep the streak going and maintain consistency in completing tasks.

These are just some of the many effective productivity techniques available. The key is to find the ones that work best for you and incorporate them into your daily routine. By adopting these techniques, you can increase focus, manage time efficiently, and achieve more in less time. Remember to also prioritize self-care and take breaks when needed to avoid burnout and maintain long-term productivity.

Chapter 4
Communication Skills

Effective verbal communication

Effective verbal communication is the ability to convey messages clearly and accurately through spoken language. It is a fundamental part of our daily interactions and is crucial to building strong relationships, expressing feelings and ideas, and achieving business goals. In today's fast-paced and diverse world, effective verbal communication has become an essential skill that can make or break success in both personal and professional contexts.

To begin with, effective verbal communication requires effective listening. Active listening is the foundation of good communication, and it involves paying close attention to what the other person is saying, asking relevant questions, and being empathetic. It is important to listen not only to the words being spoken but also to the tone of voice, body language, and emotions conveyed. This can help you understand the message in its entirety and respond appropriately.

Moreover, effective verbal communication involves speaking clearly and confidently. This means using appropriate language, tone, and volume to convey your message. It is important to speak at a pace that is comfortable for the listener, avoiding speaking too fast or too slow. Using proper grammar and avoiding slang and jargon can also help ensure your message is clear and easily understood by others. Additionally, speaking confidently and with conviction can help capture the attention of the audience and convey credibility and authority.

Furthermore, non-verbal communication plays a significant role in effective verbal communication and can sometimes convey more than the words being spoken. It includes body language, facial expressions, eye contact, and gestures. For instance, maintaining eye contact while speaking can convey sincerity and confidence, while slouching or avoiding eye contact can give the impression of disinterest or lack of confidence. Being mindful of your non-verbal cues and using them to support your words can greatly enhance your verbal communication.

Additionally, effective verbal communication involves being aware of cultural and social differences. In today's globalized world, people with different cultural backgrounds and communication styles interact regularly, and being mindful of these differences is critical for effective communication. It is important to be respectful of others' cultural norms and adapt your language and communication style accordingly. This can prevent misunderstandings, build trust, and strengthen relationships.

Furthermore, being mindful of the purpose and audience of your communication can greatly impact its effectiveness. In a professional context, for example, communication will vary depending on whether you are speaking to colleagues, superiors, or clients. Understanding the purpose and audience will help you tailor your language, tone, and style to effectively convey your message and achieve your goals.

conclusively, effective verbal communication is a crucial skill that is essential for success in both personal and professional relationships. It requires active listening, clear and confident speaking, understanding non-verbal cues, being mindful of cultural and social differences, and adapting to the purpose and audience of communication. By continuously working on and improving our verbal communication skills, we can build stronger relationships, facilitate better understanding, and achieve our goals with ease.

Importance of clear and concise communication

Clear and concise communication is an essential aspect of our everyday lives. Whether it is in our personal relationships or professional interactions, effective communication plays a crucial role in conveying ideas, exchanging information, and building strong connections. In today's fast-paced world where individuals are constantly bombarded with information, it has become more important than ever to communicate in a clear and concise manner. In this essay, we will discuss the significance of clear and concise communication and how it impacts our daily lives.

Effective communication is the foundation of any successful relationship, whether it is personal, work related, or even within our communities. Misunderstandings, conflicts, and chaos can arise when communication is unclear, leading to a breakdown in relationships and hindering progress. In personal relationships, clear and concise communication helps to establish trust and understanding, leading to more meaningful and fulfilling connections. It allows individuals to express their thoughts and feelings openly and honestly, promoting better understanding and empathy.

In a professional setting, clear and concise communication is key to achieving organizational goals. In a workplace, individuals from different backgrounds, cultures, and experiences come together to work towards a common objective. Effective communication ensures that everyone is on the same page, leading to smoother operations, increased productivity, and a positive work environment. It also helps in avoiding misunderstandings and promoting teamwork, which is vital for the success of any organization.

In addition, clear and concise communication is essential for exchanging information. Whether it is giving a presentation, writing a report, or discussing a project, the ability to communicate clearly and concisely ensures that the message is understood by the audience. It helps to convey complex ideas in a simple and understandable way, making it easier for the other party to absorb the information. This is especially important in fields such as education, where effective communication is crucial for students to learn and understand new concepts.

Moreover, in today's digital age, clear and concise communication has become more crucial than ever. With the rise of social media, emails, and messaging platforms, our written communication has become the primary means of interacting with others. In these settings, it is essential to be clear and concise in our communication as there is no tone or body language to convey our message. A simple misunderstanding or a poorly worded message can have significant consequences, whether it is a misinterpretation or a damaged reputation.

In the business world, clear and concise communication is also essential in promoting a company's brand image. Whether it is through marketing campaigns, advertisements, or social media posts, it is vital to convey the message accurately, positively, and in a concise manner. Clear communication helps to build trust with customers, enhances the company's credibility, and helps to establish a strong brand reputation.

In summary, clear and concise communication plays a crucial role in our daily lives. It helps to establish and maintain relationships, promotes efficiency and productivity, and ensures the smooth exchange of information. Furthermore, it is essential in the digital age where written communication has become the primary means of interaction. Being able to communicate clearly and concisely shows respect for the other person's time and enhances mutual understanding and respect. Therefore, it is crucial to strive for clear and concise communication in all aspects of our lives.

Tips for improving verbal communication skills

Verbal communication is an essential aspect of our daily lives, whether it's in personal or professional settings. Effective verbal communication skills help individuals convey their thoughts, ideas, and feelings clearly and confidently, leading to stronger relationships, effective collaborations, and better career opportunities. Some people are naturally good at verbal communication, while others may struggle with it. However, with practice, anyone can improve their verbal communication skills significantly. Here are some tips that can help individuals enhance their verbal communication skills.

Listen actively: Active listening is a crucial aspect of effective verbal communication. It involves paying attention to the person speaking, understanding their perspective, and responding appropriately. To be an active listener, one must maintain eye contact, avoid any distractions, and provide verbal and nonverbal cues to show attentiveness. Active listening also involves understanding the speaker's tone, body language, and emotions to get the complete message they are trying to convey.

Speak clearly and confidently: The way we speak plays a crucial role in how our message is perceived by others. To improve verbal communication skills, one must speak slowly, enunciate words clearly, and use appropriate vocabulary and grammar. Speaking with confidence also adds weight to the message being conveyed. Individuals can practice speaking in front of a mirror or record themselves to identify areas that need improvement.

Be aware of body language:
Communication is not just about words; our body language also plays a vital role in conveying our message. Nonverbal cues like eye contact, posture, gestures, and facial expressions can significantly impact the effectiveness of verbal communication. For instance, maintaining good eye contact shows confidence and interest, while slouching can make one appear disinterested. Being aware of one's body language and practicing to control it can go a long way in improving verbal communication skills.

Use supporting materials: Visual aids, such as presentations, graphs, or videos, can make verbal communication more effective. They help individuals add visual elements to their message, making it easier for the audience to understand and retain the information. However, one must ensure that the supporting materials are relevant, simple, and not overwhelming, as they can distract from the main message.

Understand the audience: Communication is a two-way process, and one must understand their audience to ensure effective communication. Different situations and individuals require different communication styles. For instance, a presentation to a group of fellow professionals may require a formal tone, while talking to friends or family may be more informal. Similarly, understanding the audience's knowledge and interest in the topic can help determine the level of detail and complexity in communication.

Practice active voice: Using active voice in verbal communication makes the message more clear and to the point. Active voice sentences are more direct, assertive, and engaging than passive voice ones. For instance, saying "I completed the project" is more effective than "The project was completed by me." Active voice also helps avoid ambiguity and confusion in communication.

Ask questions: Sometimes, individuals may not be clear about the message being conveyed, and asking questions can help clarify doubts. Asking relevant and meaningful questions can also show the speaker that the listener is interested and engaged in the conversation. However, one must ensure that the questions are not too many or interrupt the speaker's flow, as it can be distracting.

Seek feedback: Seeking feedback from others can help individuals identify areas that need improvement and gain insights into their verbal communication skills. One can ask a trusted friend or colleague to observe and provide constructive criticism on their verbal communication skills. This feedback can help individuals work on their weaknesses and become better communicators.

Verbal communication skills are essential for building relationships, advancing in one's career, and overall personal growth. With these tips, anyone can improve their verbal communication skills significantly.

Active listening

Active listening is a skill to truly hear what another person is saying, and to understand and respond appropriately. It involves being fully focused on the speaker, and giving them your undivided attention. This means not just hearing the words that are being said, but also understanding the emotions and thoughts behind them. Active listening is a crucial skill in both personal and professional relationships, as it allows for effective communication and building of strong connections.

The first step to active listening is paying attention. This means being fully present in the conversation and avoiding any distractions or interruptions. It requires giving the speaker your complete focus, and showing them through your body language, such as maintaining eye contact and nodding, that you are actively engaged in the conversation.

The next step is to show the speaker that you are listening by using verbal and nonverbal cues. Nonverbal cues, such as maintaining an open and relaxed posture, nodding, and making appropriate facial expressions, convey to the speaker that you are attentive and interested in what they have to say. Verbal cues involve using short words or phrases, such as "mm-hmm" or "I see", to encourage the speaker to continue and to show that you are understanding their message.

Another key aspect of active listening is to avoid making assumptions or interrupting the speaker. This can be challenging, as our minds naturally tend to jump to conclusions or to think about our response while someone else is speaking. However, by actively listening, we allow the speaker to fully express their thoughts and feelings without feeling rushed or unheard. Interrupting the speaker can also be seen as disrespectful and can hinder the flow of the conversation.

One of the most important elements of active listening is to ask open-ended questions. These are questions that cannot be answered with a simple "yes" or "no", and require the speaker to elaborate and provide more information. This not only shows the speaker that you are interested in what they have to say, but also helps to clarify any misunderstandings and deepen the conversation.

Reflective listening is also a crucial aspect of active listening. This involves summarizing what the speaker has said to ensure that you have understood their message correctly. This not only shows the speaker that you are actively listening, but also allows for any discrepancies or misunderstandings to be addressed and resolved.

Active listening also involves empathy and understanding the speaker's perspective. By putting yourself in the speaker's shoes and trying to understand their thoughts and feelings, you are better able to connect with them and respond appropriately. This is especially important in situations where there may be disagreements or differing opinions.

Active listening is a skill that requires practice and dedication, but it is essential for effective communication and building strong relationships. By being fully present, using verbal and nonverbal cues, avoiding assumptions and interruptions, asking open-ended questions, and showing empathy, one can become a better active listener and have more meaningful and productive conversations.

Understanding the importance of active listening

Active listening is a crucial skill that is essential for effective communication in both personal and professional settings. It is the ability to fully concentrate on what the other person is saying, understand their perspective, and respond in a way that shows genuine interest and understanding. Active listening involves more than just hearing the words being spoken; it requires active participation and engagement, as well as the capacity to understand the underlying message being conveyed.

In today's fast-paced world, where distractions are abundant, active listening has become increasingly important. It is a skill that is underrated but is essential for building strong relationships, both personal and professional. Here are some reasons why understanding the importance of active listening is crucial:

Builds trust and rapport:
Active listening helps in building trust and rapport between individuals. When a person feels heard and understood, they are more likely to open up and share their thoughts and feelings. When this happens, it creates a strong bond between the individuals, leading to a deeper connection and understanding.

Enhances communication:
Active listening is a two-way process that involves not only listening to what is being said but also providing a response. It encourages a deeper level of communication, allowing people to express

their thoughts and ideas clearly and effectively. This, in turn, helps to avoid misunderstandings and promotes a more productive exchange of information.

Resolves conflicts:

Conflicts are a natural part of any relationship, whether personal or professional. However, active listening can be a powerful tool in resolving conflicts. When individuals practice active listening, they try to understand the other person's perspective, which can lead to finding common ground and working towards a mutually beneficial solution.

Improves problem-solving:

Active listening is a vital aspect of effective problem-solving. When individuals listen actively, they gather all the necessary information, and this helps them to analyze the situation better. With a deeper understanding of the problem, better solutions can be found, and decisions can be made more efficiently.

Boosts empathy and understanding:

Active listening requires one to be fully present in the conversation and to put oneself in the speaker's shoes. This helps individuals to develop empathy towards the other person and understand their point of view. Being empathetic allows people to connect better with others and helps to build stronger relationships.

Encourages personal growth:
Not only does active listening benefit relationships, but it also promotes personal growth. When individuals focus on actively listening, they learn more about themselves and others. They learn how to communicate effectively and understand different perspectives, which helps in personal and professional development.

Increases knowledge and learning:
Active listening allows people to gain new information, perspectives, and insights. It helps to broaden one's understanding of different subjects and situations. By actively listening, individuals can also learn to question and challenge their own opinions and beliefs, leading to personal growth and continuous learning.

In conclusion, active listening is an important skill that promotes effective communication, builds trust and empathy, and enhances personal and professional relationships. It goes beyond just hearing what someone is saying, and requires individuals to be fully engaged and attentive. By understanding the importance of active listening, one can improve their communication skills, build stronger relationships, and achieve personal and professional growth.

Techniques for active listening

Active listening is a communication technique that involves paying full attention to the speaker and responding in a way that shows understanding and interest. It goes beyond just hearing the words being spoken; it requires the listener to make a conscious effort to understand the message being conveyed, both verbally and nonverbally. Active listening is a valuable skill that can improve relationships, build trust, and enhance communication. Here are some techniques for active listening:

Give Undivided Attention: The first step in active listening is to pay complete attention to the speaker. This means putting away distractions such as phones, laptops, or other things that might divide your focus. Make eye contact, face the speaker, and avoid interrupting them while they are speaking.

Show Nonverbal Cues: Nonverbal cues such as nodding, smiling, maintaining an open posture, and making appropriate facial expressions show that you are listening and engaged. This gives the speaker the confidence to continue expressing their thoughts and feelings.

Use Verbal Cues: In addition to nonverbal cues, using verbal cues such as "I see," "I understand," "That's interesting," or "Tell me more" can also encourage the speaker to share more. These cues also show that you are actively listening and interested in what the speaker has to say.

Paraphrase: Paraphrasing is an effective technique where the listener restates what the speaker has said in their own words. This not only shows that you are listening but also helps to clarify any misunderstandings. For example, "What I hear you saying is..." or "Let me make sure I understand correctly..."

Reflect Feelings: Active listening involves paying attention to the speaker's tone and body language as well. Reflecting their feelings back to them can help the speaker feel heard and understood. For example, "It sounds like you are feeling frustrated," or "It seems like you are really excited about this."

Ask Open-Ended Questions: Asking open-ended questions encourages the speaker to elaborate and provide more details, which can lead to a deeper understanding of their thoughts and feelings. Avoid closed-ended questions that can be answered with a simple yes or no.

Use Silence: Sometimes, the speaker needs a moment to collect their thoughts or process their emotions. In these moments, it is important to remain silent and give them time to think. Silence can also be used to show that you are listening and that the speaker has your full attention.

Avoid Judgment: Active listening means being non-judgmental and setting aside your own opinions and biases. When we listen without judgment, we create a safe and open environment for the speaker to express themselves freely.

Summarize: As the conversation progresses, it is helpful to periodically summarize what has been said to ensure a mutual understanding. This also allows the speaker to clarify any points that may have been misunderstood or left out.

Practice Empathy: Empathy is the ability to put yourself in someone else's shoes and understand their perspective. It is essential for active listening as it allows you to see things from the speaker's point of view and helps to build trust and rapport.

Conclusively, active listening requires conscious effort and practice to master. By following these techniques, you can become a better active listener and improve the quality of your communication and relationships. With active listening, you not only show respect and understanding for the speaker but also gain valuable insights and build stronger connections.

Non-verbal communication

Non-verbal communication plays a crucial role in our daily interactions, whether we are consciously aware of it or not. It refers to any form of communication that does not involve words or verbal language. This can include body language, facial expressions, tone of voice, gestures, posture, and even silence. Non-verbal cues are universal and can convey messages without the need for language, making it an essential part of human communication.

One of the primary functions of non-verbal communication is to complement, emphasize, or modify the message being conveyed through spoken words. The use of gestures, facial expressions, and tone of voice can add layers of meaning to what is being said. For example, a simple nod can indicate agreement, while a frown could convey disagreement without the need for words. Similarly, a sarcastic tone of voice can alter the meaning of a message entirely.

Non-verbal communication also plays a significant role in expressing emotions. Our facial expressions, posture, and tone of voice can reveal our feelings and attitudes towards a particular person or situation. For instance, a smile can indicate happiness, while a frown can signal displeasure. These non-verbal cues can be more reliable indicators of true emotions compared to verbal language, which can be easily manipulated.

Furthermore, non-verbal communication helps establish and maintain relationships. The use of eye contact, physical touch, and personal space can convey trust, intimacy, and closeness. For example, a warm and firm handshake can communicate confidence and trust, while a hug can express affection and care. The lack of these non-verbal cues can also indicate discomfort, avoidance, or hostility in a relationship.

Non-verbal communication also varies across cultures, with different gestures and expressions having different meanings. For instance, a thumbs-up gesture may mean approval in Western cultures, but it can be considered rude in other cultures. Therefore, it is essential to understand cultural norms and adapt to them when communicating with people from different backgrounds.

In addition to complementing verbal communication, non-verbal cues also serve as a substitute for words in situations where communication is not possible. For example, people with hearing impairments use sign language to communicate, and actors use body language and facial expressions to convey emotions on stage. In these instances, non-verbal cues become the primary means of communication.

Non-verbal communication also encompasses our appearance, including clothing, hairstyle, and body modifications. These visual cues can reveal our social status, personality, and cultural background. Our appearance can also influence how others perceive and interact with us, making it an important aspect of non-verbal communication.

In conclusion, non-verbal communication is a powerful tool that complements and enhances verbal language in our daily interactions. It helps us express emotions, establish relationships, and convey messages without the need for words. Understanding and effectively using non-verbal cues can improve our communication skills and enable us to connect with others on a deeper level.

Types of non-verbal communication

Non-verbal communication is the process of conveying meaning through non-verbal cues such as facial expressions, body movements, gestures, and tone of voice. It is an essential part of human communication and often carries a more significant impact than verbal communication. There are multiple types of non-verbal communication, which can vary across cultures and contexts.

Facial expressions: Facial expressions are a vital aspect of non-verbal communication and involve the use of the face to convey emotions and intentions. The most common facial expressions are happiness, sadness, anger, fear, surprise, and disgust. For example, a smile can convey friendliness, while a frown can indicate disapproval.

Body language: Body language involves the use of postures and movements to communicate. It includes gestures, such as nodding, hand movements, and the positioning of arms and legs. Body language can also convey attitudes and emotions, such as standing with crossed arms, which can indicate defensiveness or closed-off behavior.

Eye contact: Eye contact is an essential type of non-verbal communication that involves looking directly into someone's eyes while speaking or listening. It conveys interest, attention, and sincerity in a conversation. However, eye contact can also vary across cultures, and prolonged eye contact can be interpreted as aggressive or disrespectful in some cultures.

Paralanguage: Paralanguage refers to the tone, pitch, and volume of the voice. It can convey emotions, attitudes, and emphasis. For example, raising the tone of voice can indicate excitement or anger, while lowering the pitch can convey sadness or seriousness.

Proxemics: Proxemics refers to the use of personal space and distance in communication. Different cultures have different norms and expectations regarding personal space, and violating these norms can result in discomfort or offense. For example, in some cultures, standing too close to someone while speaking can be considered intrusive, while in others, it can indicate trust and closeness.

Touch: Touch is a powerful form of non-verbal communication that involves physical contact with another person. It can convey a range of emotions, such as affection, comfort, or aggression. The meaning of touch can also vary across cultures, and what may be acceptable in one culture may be deemed inappropriate in another.

Appearance: The way we dress and present ourselves can also convey non-verbal cues. Our clothing, hairstyle, and grooming can communicate information about our personality, social status, and culture. For example, a person wearing a suit is often perceived as professional and responsible, while a person wearing casual attire may be seen as laid-back or approachable.

Symbols and objects: Non-verbal communication can also be conveyed through the use of symbols and objects. For instance, a peace sign or a thumbs-up can communicate a specific message without any words being spoken. Similarly, a handshake can convey trust, while a nodding or shaking head can indicate agreement or disagreement.

Non-verbal communication plays a crucial role in our daily interactions and can significantly impact the meaning and effectiveness of our communication. It is essential to be mindful of these various types of non-verbal cues and understand how they can vary across cultures to effectively communicate with others.

How to use non-verbal cues effectively

Non-verbal communication is a powerful way to express thoughts, feelings, and emotions without using words. It includes body language, facial expressions, gestures, posture, and tone of voice. Non-verbal cues can convey more information than spoken words and can often be more influential in a conversation.

Therefore, learning to use non-verbal cues effectively can greatly improve our communication skills and help us better connect with others.

Here are some tips on how to use non-verbal cues effectively:

Be aware of your body language: The first step to using non-verbal cues effectively is to be aware of your body language. Your body language can convey a lot of information, even if you are not aware of it. Therefore, make sure to maintain a relaxed and confident posture. Stand straight, make eye contact, and avoid slouching or fidgeting.

Match your non-verbal cues with your words: It is important to make sure that your verbal and non-verbal cues are aligned. This means that your body language should match the words you are saying. For example, if you are talking about something exciting, your voice should be enthusiastic, and your body language should be energetic and animated.

Use facial expressions: Your face is one of the most expressive parts of your body. Smiling, frowning, raising your eyebrows, or making other facial expressions can convey your emotions and add meaning to your words. Smiling, in particular, can make you seem more approachable and friendly.

Pay attention to tone and pitch: The way you say something is just as important as what you say. Your tone of voice and pitch can convey different emotions and can greatly influence the meaning of your words. For example, saying "I am fine" with a cheerful tone and saying the same words with a sarcastic tone can completely change the message you are trying to convey.

Use gestures: Gestures can add emphasis and clarity to your words. They can also help you better express yourself and make your message more engaging. However, it is important to use gestures sparingly and avoid being too dramatic or distracting.

Consider the cultural context: It is important to be aware that non-verbal cues can vary greatly across cultures. What may be considered appropriate in one culture may be considered offensive in another. Therefore, it is crucial to be mindful of cultural differences and adjust your non-verbal cues accordingly.

Pay attention to the non-verbal cues of others: Effective communication is a two-way process. Therefore, it is important to pay attention to the non-verbal cues of others. This can help you understand their feelings and thoughts better and adjust your own non-verbal cues accordingly. For example, if someone seems to be uncomfortable, you can try to make them feel more at ease by using open and welcoming body language.

Generally, non-verbal cues can greatly enhance our communication skills and help us better connect with others. It is important to be aware of our body language, use facial expressions and gestures, and pay attention to tone and pitch when communicating. By practicing and being mindful of cultural differences, we can use non-verbal cues effectively and improve the effectiveness of our communication.

Chapter 5
Networking and Building Relationships

Networking and building relationships are essential components in both personal and professional development. It is a process of creating and maintaining mutually beneficial connections with others, which can lead to opportunities, growth, and success.

In today's fast-paced and competitive world, networking has become more important than ever. It is a way to expand our circle and make new connections, which can open doors to new opportunities and collaborations. Building relationships, on the other hand, involves nurturing and maintaining these connections through meaningful interactions and mutual trust.

The benefits of networking and building relationships are numerous. They provide us with a support system and a sense of community, where we can share our ideas, seek advice and grow together. It allows us to learn from others, gain different perspectives, and widen our horizons.

Moreover, networking and building relationships are crucial for professional growth. By connecting with people in our industry or related fields, we can gain valuable insights, stay updated with the latest trends, and potentially find job opportunities. Building strong relationships with colleagues, mentors, and industry leaders can also help us advance in our career.

Networking and building relationships also play a vital role in entrepreneurship and business success. By creating a strong network and building genuine relationships with potential clients, partners, and investors, entrepreneurs can expand their business, gain new clients and secure funding.

However, networking and building relationships require effort, time, and consistency. It is essential to have a clear goal and purpose in mind while networking, whether it is to find a new job, grow your business or learn from industry experts. A genuine interest in others and the willingness to help and contribute to their success is also important in building meaningful relationships.

Here are some tips for effective networking and building relationships:

- Attend networking events, conferences, and workshops in your field of interest.
- Use social media platforms like LinkedIn to connect with professionals and stay updated with industry news and events.
- Be open-minded and curious about others. Ask questions and actively listen to their responses.
- Offer value to others by sharing your knowledge, skills, or connections.
- Follow up with people after networking events and maintain regular communication.
- Show gratitude and appreciation for the people in your network by acknowledging their contributions and achievements.
- Be genuine and authentic in your interactions, and avoid being solely driven by self-interest.

In conclusion, networking and building relationships are crucial for personal and professional growth. By expanding our network, nurturing our connections, and being genuinely invested in others' success, we can open doors to new opportunities, gain valuable insights, and build a strong support system.

Importance of networking

Networking plays a crucial role in today's interconnected world. It involves creating and maintaining professional relationships with people in your industry and beyond. It is essential for both personal and professional growth as it provides a platform to exchange ideas, resources, and support. In today's competitive market, networking has become a powerful tool for success, and here are some reasons why networking is essential.

Building Connections: Networking allows individuals to build meaningful connections with people from diverse backgrounds and industries. It provides a platform to meet potential clients, partners, and mentors who can help in the growth of one's career or business. Moreover, these connections can lead to future opportunities and partnerships.

Sharing Ideas and Knowledge: Through networking, individuals can share their knowledge and expertise with others. It provides a space for like-minded individuals to discuss industry trends, share valuable insights, and learn from one another's experiences. This exchange of ideas can lead to new perspectives, innovative solutions, and can help in keeping up with the changing industry landscape.

Career Advancement: Networking is crucial for career advancement as it allows individuals to expand their professional circle. Through networking events and platforms, individuals can connect with industry leaders, potential employers, and recruiters. This can open doors to new job opportunities, internships, and promotions.

Continuous Learning: By networking with professionals from different backgrounds, individuals can gain knowledge about diverse industries and fields. This continuous learning can help individuals expand their skill set, broaden their horizons, and make them more valuable in the job market.

Access to Resources: Networking provides access to valuable resources such as industry insights, mentoring, and knowledge sharing. It also allows individuals to tap into the networks of their connections, which can provide access to resources such as funding, partnerships, and support.

Boosting Confidence and Visibility: Networking allows individuals to step out of their comfort zone and interact with new people. It helps in developing social and communication skills, which are crucial for personal and professional growth. It also increases visibility and helps individuals establish themselves as an authority in their field.

Opportunities for Collaboration: Through networking, individuals can find like-minded individuals and potential collaborators for business or personal projects. By joining forces, individuals can share resources, skills, and knowledge, leading to mutual growth and success.

Support System: Networking also provides a support system in the form of mentors, peers, and friends. These relationships can provide guidance, motivation, and emotional support in times of need, especially for individuals starting their careers or businesses.

Networking is a vital aspect of personal and professional development. It opens doors to new opportunities, resources, and support, which are crucial for success and growth in today's interconnected world. By investing time and effort in networking, individuals can expand their horizons, build meaningful connections, and achieve their goals.

Benefits of networking for success

Social networking has taken the world by storm, connecting people from all walks of life and industries. With the advancement of technology, networking has evolved from personal interactions to virtual platforms. Today, networking has become an essential tool for achieving success in both personal and professional endeavors. It offers a wide range of benefits that can greatly impact individuals and their careers. In this essay, we will explore the various benefits of networking for success.

Expands professional connections:
Networking is all about building and maintaining relationships. When individuals attend networking events or connect with others on social media platforms, they have the opportunity to meet new people and expand their professional connections. These connections can open doors to new career opportunities, collaborations, referrals, and even mentorship.

Opportunities for growth and learning:
Networking provides a platform for individuals to learn from other professionals

in their field or industry. Through interactions with others, they can gain insights and knowledge about current trends, best practices, and new technologies. Additionally, networking events often have speakers who share valuable insights and experiences that can inspire and motivate individuals towards success.

Builds confidence and communication skills: Networking allows individuals to interact with people from different backgrounds, cultures, and industries. This opens the door for individuals to improve their communication and social skills. As individuals attend more networking events, they become more comfortable and confident in striking up conversations and presenting their ideas. These skills are vital for success, especially in the business world.

Increases visibility and exposure: Through networking, individuals can increase their visibility and exposure within their industry. When they attend conferences, seminars, or other networking events, they have the opportunity to showcase their skills, knowledge, and expertise. This can lead to new business opportunities, job offers, or speaking engagements. Furthermore, by sharing content on social media platforms, individuals can reach a wider audience and establish their personal brand.

Provides a support system: Networking creates a support system for individuals, especially in the business world. By connecting with like-minded individuals, they can share their challenges, seek advice, and receive support from others who have faced similar struggles. This support system can be a valuable resource for individuals looking to advance in their careers.

Access to new perspectives and ideas: Networking provides individuals with the chance to exchange ideas and perspectives with others. This exposure to diverse viewpoints can challenge their thinking and lead to new insights and ideas. This can be beneficial in problem-solving, decision-making, and fostering creativity and innovation.

Opens new business opportunities: In today's highly competitive business world, building a network is essential for success. A vast network can introduce individuals to new business opportunities, such as partnerships, collaborations, and potential clients. It can also lead to potential investors or funding for entrepreneurial ventures.

Boosts self-confidence: Networking activities, such as public speaking and interacting with new people, can be intimidating for some individuals. However, as they attend more events and interact with others, they will build their self-confidence. This can have a significant impact on their personal and professional growth and success.

Access to resources and information: Networking provides individuals with access to valuable resources and information. By connecting with professionals in their industry, they can gain insights about new job opportunities, industry trends, and developments. This can help individuals stay updated, enhance their knowledge and skills, and stay ahead in their careers.

In summary, networking has become an essential tool for achieving success in today's society. The benefits of networking are not limited to personal growth but extend to career advancement and business success. It offers individuals the chance to build valuable relationships, learn from others, increase visibility, gain new perspectives, and access resources and information. Therefore, individuals should actively engage in networking activities to reap these benefits and achieve their goals and aspirations.

Techniques for effective networking

Networking is an essential tool for building and maintaining professional relationships, expanding career opportunities, and nurturing personal growth. It involves connecting and interacting with people from different backgrounds, industries, and professions. Effective networking can lead to valuable connections, potential job opportunities, and can accelerate career growth. However, networking is not just about meeting and collecting business cards or adding people on social media. It requires dedication, effort, and proper strategy to achieve success. In this article, we will discuss some techniques for effective networking.

Be approachable and genuine:

The first and foremost technique for effective networking is to be approachable and authentic. People are more likely to engage and interact with individuals who are friendly and genuine. When attending networking events or meetings, smile, make eye contact, and introduce yourself confidently. Be open to conversations and show interest in others. Remember to be genuine and avoid being too pushy or only talking about yourself.

Identify your networking goals:

Before you start networking, it is crucial to know your goals. Are you seeking career advice, looking for a new job, or expanding your professional connections? Knowing your goals will help you focus on your approach and the kind of connections you want to make. It will also help you identify relevant networking events and potential contacts.

Attend in-person and virtual events:

Networking events are a great way to meet like-minded professionals and build connections. In-person events provide an opportunity to establish a personal connection and build rapport, while virtual events are more convenient and can connect you with people from anywhere in the world. Attend a mix of both to broaden your reach and interact with a diverse group of people.

Join professional networking groups:

There are several networking groups focused on particular industries, professions, or interests. Joining these groups can be beneficial for expanding your connections and increasing your knowledge in a specific field. These groups may organize events, workshops, or online forums to facilitate meaningful networking.

Use social media:

In the digital age, social media has become a powerful tool for networking. Platforms like LinkedIn, Twitter, and Facebook allow you to connect with professionals from all over the world. Join professional groups, follow industry leaders, and engage in conversations to build your network. Remember to maintain a professional image on your social media profiles, as it can be a reflection of you as a professional.

Follow up and maintain relationships:

Effective networking is not just about meeting new people; it is also about maintaining relationships. After meeting someone, follow up with an email or a message to thank them for their time and express your interest in staying connected. It is essential to keep in touch with your connections regularly. Follow them on social media, send them articles or information that may be relevant to their interests, and offer your help or support when needed.

Be a resource for others:

Networking is a two-way street. It is not just about what you can gain from others, but also what you can offer. Be a resource for others by sharing your knowledge, expertise, or resources. Offer to connect people in your network who may benefit from meeting each other. By being a resource for others, you establish yourself as a valuable contact, and people will be more likely to turn to you for help or advice.

Follow-up offline:

While online networking is convenient, meeting someone in person is more impactful. After connecting with someone through social media or email, try to meet them in person for a coffee or lunch. This will allow you to deepen your connection and build a stronger relationship.

In conclusion, networking is a critical aspect of personal and professional growth. By following these techniques and actively engaging in networking, you can expand your reach, build meaningful connections, and accelerate your career growth. Remember to be genuine, have clear goals, maintain relationships, and be a resource for others. With consistent effort and a strategic approach, you can become an effective networker and open doors to new opportunities.

Building and maintaining relationships

Building and maintaining relationships is an essential aspect of life for people of all ages and backgrounds. Relationships can take many forms, such as family bonds, friendships, romantic partnerships, and professional connections. Good relationships are beneficial for our overall well-being and can enrich our lives in various ways.

Here are some key points to consider when building and maintaining relationships:

Communication: Effective communication is the foundation of any relationship. It is vital to listen actively, express yourself clearly, and be honest and open with your thoughts and feelings. Good communication helps in understanding each other and resolving conflicts.

Trust: Trust is a crucial element in any relationship. It takes time and effort to build trust, and it can be easily broken. Being consistent, keeping promises, and being reliable can help in fostering trust in a relationship.

Respect: Showing respect for others is essential in building and maintaining healthy relationships. This includes respecting each other's boundaries, opinions, and feelings. When one feels respected, they are more likely to reciprocate and maintain a positive relationship.

Empathy: Empathy is the ability to understand and share the feelings of another person. It allows us to connect with others on a deeper level and helps in building a strong emotional bond. Practicing empathy can also help in resolving conflicts and strengthening relationships.

Compromise: No two individuals are the same, and disagreements are inevitable in any relationship. Learning to compromise and find a middle ground can help in avoiding conflicts and maintaining harmony in a relationship.

Quality time: Spending quality time together is crucial in building and maintaining relationships. Making an effort to prioritize and dedicate time to the people in your life shows them that they are valued and strengthens the bond between you.

Conflict resolution: Conflicts are a natural part of any relationship, and learning how to resolve them respectfully and effectively is essential. Communication, empathy, and compromise are key components of conflict resolution.

Appreciation: Showing appreciation and expressing gratitude for the people in our lives is vital in maintaining positive relationships. It can be as simple as saying thank you or acknowledging their efforts. These small gestures make others feel valued and appreciated.

Forgiveness: No one is perfect, and everyone makes mistakes. Learning to forgive and move on is crucial in maintaining healthy relationships. Holding onto resentment and grudges can damage relationships and lead to further conflicts.

Consistency: Consistency is vital in any relationship. It involves showing up, keeping promises, and being reliable. When people know they can count on you, it strengthens the foundation of your relationship.

Building and maintaining relationships takes time, effort, and commitment from both parties. It involves good communication, trust, respect, empathy, compromise, and appreciation. By practicing these traits, we can create and nurture strong and fulfilling relationships with the people in our lives.

Importance of relationships in success

Relationships are crucial for success in every aspect of life, be it personal or professional. Our success is not solely dependent on our own efforts and talents, but also on the support and collaboration of others. Building and nurturing meaningful relationships is crucial for achieving success and here's why:

Networking and Connections: In today's highly competitive world, networking and building connections is essential for success. Connecting with people from different backgrounds and industries can open doors to new opportunities, ideas, and resources. Strong relationships can provide valuable insights, advice, and referrals, making it easier to achieve our goals and reach new heights.

Support and Motivation: Success is not a solitary journey. We all need support and motivation from time to time, and that's where relationships play a vital role. Having a strong support system of friends, family, mentors, and colleagues can keep us motivated, offer guidance during tough times and celebrate our victories with us. They can also provide constructive criticism and help us stay accountable for our actions, making us more determined towards achieving success.

Learning and Growth: Relationships help us expand our knowledge and skills. By interacting and collaborating with different people, we gain new perspectives, ideas, and learn from their experiences and expertise. Whether it's a mentor or a friend, relationships provide an opportunity for growth and continuous learning, which are essential for success in today's dynamic world.

Teamwork and Collaboration: In today's interconnected world, success rarely comes from working alone. Successful individuals understand the importance of teamwork and building relationships with their team members. By developing positive relationships with our colleagues and team members, we create a supportive and collaborative work environment where everyone can contribute their best and achieve success together.

Self-Reflection and Personal Development: Relationships also play a crucial role in our personal development. The people we spend time with influence our thoughts, behaviors, and choices. Healthy relationships help us become more self-aware, identify our strengths and weaknesses, and work on improving ourselves to become the best version of ourselves. This self-reflection and personal development are vital for achieving success in all areas of life.

Networking Opportunities: Building relationships not only helps us in our personal and professional lives but also presents us with networking opportunities. Attending social gatherings, conferences, and events provide an excellent platform to build new relationships, establish new connections, and extend our network, which can prove to be valuable for our success.

Relationships are imperative for success, as they provide us support, motivation, learning opportunities, and collaborative environments. They act as a support system, provide us with useful connections, help us grow as individuals, and present us with new opportunities. Therefore, investing time and effort in building and nurturing meaningful relationships can significantly contribute to our success in all aspects of life.

Ways to build and nurture meaningful relationships

Building and nurturing meaningful relationships is essential for our overall happiness and well-being. Humans are inherently social beings and crave connection with others. Meaningful relationships provide a sense of belonging, support, and understanding, and can greatly enrich our lives. However, building and nurturing these relationships requires effort, communication, and vulnerability. Here are some ways to cultivate and maintain meaningful relationships:

Be a good listener: One of the foundations of a meaningful relationship is being a good listener. This means actively listening to what the other person is saying, without interrupting or judging. Show empathy and ask questions to understand their perspective. When people feel heard and understood, it strengthens the bond between them.

Communicate clearly and openly: Communication is crucial in any relationship, but it's especially important in meaningful ones. Be honest and open about your thoughts, feelings, and needs. Avoid making assumptions and be willing to have difficult conversations. Good communication can help prevent misunderstandings and conflicts from damaging the relationship.

Show appreciation and gratitude: Taking the time to express appreciation and gratitude for each other can go a long way in building and nurturing a healthy relationship. It shows that you value and care for the other person. Don't take them for granted and make an effort to acknowledge the little things they do for you.

Be present and make time for each other: In today's fast-paced world, it's easy to get caught up in our busy schedules and neglect our relationships. Make a conscious effort to be present and fully engaged when spending time with your loved ones. Put away distractions like phones and television and focus on connecting and making memories.

Share experiences: Building meaningful relationships involves creating shared experiences. This can be as simple as going for a walk together, cooking a meal, or taking a trip. Doing things together creates bonds and memories that strengthen the relationship. These shared experiences also provide an opportunity for communication and getting to know each other on a deeper level.

Support each other: Meaningful relationships are a two-way street. It's important to be there for each other during both good and bad times. Offer support, encouragement, and a listening ear when the other person needs it. Show up for important events and milestones, and celebrate each other's achievements. This builds trust and strengthens the relationship.

Be yourself and accept each other: Authenticity is key in any relationship. Be true to who you are and encourage the other person to do the same. Accept each other's flaws and imperfections, and don't try to change each other. Show unconditional love and support, and create a safe space for vulnerability and honesty.

Forgive and apologize: No relationship is perfect, and conflicts are bound to happen. When they do, it's important to apologize when you're wrong and forgive when you're wronged. Holding onto grudges and resentments can damage a relationship. Learn to communicate and work through issues together, and be willing to forgive and move forward.

Respect boundaries: Each person in a relationship has their own boundaries and limits. It's important to respect these boundaries and not push someone outside of their comfort zone. Similarly, communicate your own boundaries and make sure they are respected. This creates a sense of safety and trust within the relationship.

Continuously invest in the relationship: Meaningful relationships require continuous effort and investment. Don't take the other person for granted and let the relationship become stagnant. Make an effort to do things that keep the relationship alive and growing, such as trying new things, having deep conversations, or setting shared goals.

Building and nurturing meaningful relationships takes time, effort, and vulnerability. It requires good communication, respect, and a willingness to invest in the relationship. By following these suggestions, you can cultivate strong, supportive, and fulfilling relationships that can positively impact your life. Remember, meaningful relationships are a source of joy, comfort, and growth, and they are worth the effort.

Chapter 6
Resilience and Perseverance

Resilience and Perseverance
Resilience refers to the ability to bounce back from challenging experiences or setbacks. It is the strength that allows individuals to overcome difficulties and move forward despite obstacles or failures.

Perseverance, on the other hand, is the determination to continue working towards a goal even when faced with difficulties or setbacks. It is the persistence and tenacity to keep going, even when the going gets tough.

Both resilience and perseverance are important qualities that can help individuals succeed in life. Here are some reasons why they are important:

Helps overcome challenges and setbacks.

Life is full of challenges and setbacks, and these can be difficult to navigate. However, having resilience and perseverance can help individuals overcome these obstacles and keep moving forward towards their goals.

Builds character and inner strength. Resilience and perseverance require the development of inner strength and character. By facing and overcoming challenges, individuals can develop resilience and perseverance, which can help them become stronger and more resilient in the face of future challenges.

Encourages growth and self-improvement. Both resilience and perseverance require individuals to learn from their experiences and use them to grow and improve. By facing and overcoming challenges, individuals can learn valuable lessons and develop their skills and abilities, making them more resilient and persistent in the future.

Increases chances of success.

Having resilience and perseverance can greatly increase an individual's chances of success. By not giving up and constantly working towards their goals, individuals are more likely to achieve success in their personal and professional lives.

Promotes a positive attitude.
Resilient and perseverant individuals often have a positive attitude towards life. They see challenges as opportunities for growth and are not easily discouraged by setbacks. This positive attitude can help them stay motivated and focused on their goals, even when faced with difficulties.

Inspires and motivates others.
Resilient and perseverant individuals can serve as role models for others. Seeing someone overcome challenges and achieve success can inspire and motivate others to do the same. By displaying these qualities, individuals can positively impact those around them and create a ripple effect of resilience and perseverance.

Resilience and perseverance are crucial qualities that can help individuals overcome challenges, achieve success, and inspire others. By developing these qualities, individuals can better navigate the ups and downs of life and ultimately lead more fulfilling lives.

Understanding resilience

Definition of resilience

Resilience refers to an individual's ability to adapt and bounce back from difficult and challenging situations. It involves maintaining a positive outlook, effectively managing stress and adversity, and being able to problem-solve and overcome obstacles.

Resilience is not about avoiding difficulties, but rather about having the skills and resources to face and overcome them. It is also not a fixed trait, but something that can be developed and strengthened over time.

Some key factors that contribute to resilience include having a strong support system, maintaining a positive mindset, being flexible and adaptable, having effective coping strategies, and being able to learn from past experiences and mistakes. It is also important to have a sense of self-awareness and understanding of one's own emotions and reactions.

Resilience is important because it allows individuals to bounce back quicker from setbacks, persevere through difficult times, and ultimately lead a more fulfilling and successful life. It can also help individuals better navigate and cope with future challenges and stressors.

Resilience is often associated with the concept of "toughness" or "mental toughness," but it is much more than that. It is the ability to adapt and recover from difficult experiences, to learn from them, and become stronger as a result. Resilient individuals are not immune to stress or hardships; they simply have the inner resources and skills to manage them effectively.

There are different types of resilience, such as psychological, emotional, physical, and social resilience. Psychological resilience refers to an individual's ability to cope with stressors and maintain mental well-being. Emotional resilience involves managing emotions and maintaining a sense of balance during challenging situations. Physical resilience is the ability to adapt and recover from physical challenges and illnesses. Social resilience involves developing and maintaining strong relationships and support networks.

Resilience is not something that a person either has or does not have; it is a process that can be developed and improved upon. Some people may be naturally more resilient, but everyone has the potential to become more resilient with practice and determination. Resilience is like a muscle that can be strengthened through various strategies and techniques.

Cognitive flexibility, problem-solving skills, and self-regulation are essential components of resilience. People who are resilient have the ability to see challenges as opportunities for growth and learning. They have a positive and optimistic mindset, focusing on what they can control rather than what they cannot. They also have the ability to regulate their emotions, thoughts, and behaviors in response to stressful situations, instead of being overwhelmed by them.

Moreover, resilience is not just an individual trait; it is also influenced by external factors such as family, community, and culture. The support and encouragement of family, friends, and community can play a significant role in helping individuals overcome challenges and become more resilient. Cultural beliefs and practices can also impact a person's resilience, as some cultures place a strong emphasis on community and collective resilience.

Resilience is a crucial skill in today's fast-paced and unpredictable world. With the constant changes and challenges that life brings, being resilient allows individuals to handle difficulties and setbacks with resilience. It enables them to adapt, grow, and thrive in the face of adversity.

Resilience is especially important in times of crisis, such as natural disasters, pandemics, or personal hardships.

Resilience is the ability to overcome challenges and setbacks, bounce back from adversity, and maintain a positive outlook. It is a skill that can be developed and strengthened through various strategies and techniques. Resilience is crucial for navigating through life's difficulties and emerging stronger and more empowered.

Why resilience is important for success

Resilience is defined as the ability to adapt, bounce back and recover from challenges, setbacks, and obstacles. It is an essential factor in achieving success, as it allows individuals to overcome difficulties and continue to move forward towards their goals. In today's fast-paced and constantly changing world, resilience has become more important than ever before. It is a quality that not only helps individuals to succeed in their personal and professional lives but also enables them to cope with the ever-increasing pressures of modern-day living.

One of the primary reasons why resilience is crucial for success is that it helps individuals to overcome adversity. Life is full of unexpected challenges and setbacks that can often bring people to their knees. However, those who possess resilience have the ability to bounce back from these difficult situations and come out even stronger. They do not let failures or setbacks hold them back, and instead, they view them as opportunities for growth and learning. This unwavering attitude towards challenges is what drives individuals towards success, as they do not allow themselves to be defeated by temporary setbacks.

Furthermore, resilience enables individuals to maintain a positive mindset even in the face of hardships. Having a positive outlook is crucial for success as it allows individuals to stay focused, motivated, and determined to overcome any obstacles that come their way. Resilient individuals do not allow negative thoughts or experiences to cripple their spirits but instead use them as fuel to keep moving forward. They see failures as stepping stones towards success and find ways to turn setbacks into opportunities for growth and improvement.

Moreover, resilience helps individuals to adapt to changing circumstances. In today's fast-paced world, the ability to adapt is vital for success. Flexibility and the willingness to change are essential qualities that enable individuals to stay competitive and thrive in a constantly evolving environment. Resilience allows individuals to adjust to changes, whether they are personal or professional, and find ways to make the best of the situation. This adaptability can be the determining factor between success and failure, as those who can adapt quickly and effectively are more likely to come out on top.

Another critical aspect of resilience that contributes to success is the ability to manage stress and maintain emotional stability. Today, stress is a prevalent issue that affects individuals from all walks of life. However, resilient individuals have the mental fortitude and coping skills to deal with stress effectively. They are better equipped to handle pressure, remain calm under difficult circumstances, and make rational decisions. This enables them to perform at their best and work towards achieving their goals despite any challenges they may face.

Overcoming setbacks and failures

Setbacks and failures are an inevitable part of life. No matter how successful or determined we may be, we are bound to face obstacles and experience failures along the way. These setbacks can be in the form of rejection, loss, disappointment, or any other form of adversity that hinders our progress towards our goals. While these experiences may seem difficult and demotivating, they also provide us with valuable opportunities for growth and self-improvement. Overcoming setbacks and failures is an essential skill that can help us bounce back stronger and more resilient than before.

Here are some tips on how to overcome setbacks and failures:

Embrace a positive mindset: The first step towards overcoming setbacks and failures is to adopt a positive mindset. Instead of dwelling on the negative aspects of the situation, try to find the silver lining and focus on the lessons learned. Remember that every failure brings you one step closer to success, and every setback is an opportunity to learn and grow.

Reframe your perspective: How we perceive and interpret setbacks and failures is crucial in determining how we respond to them. Rather than seeing them as a sign of personal inadequacy, view them as a chance to reassess your goals, strategies, and approach. Look at them as stepping stones towards achieving your ultimate goal, rather than roadblocks.

Learn from your mistakes: Don't shy away from acknowledging your mistakes and shortcomings. Use them as learning opportunities to avoid making the same mistakes in the future. Ask yourself what you could have done differently, and use this knowledge to improve and develop your skills.

Practice resilience: Resilience is the ability to bounce back from difficult situations and adapt to change. It is a crucial quality in overcoming setbacks and failures. To build resilience, try to maintain a positive outlook, work on your problem-solving skills, and practice self-care. Also, surround yourself with supportive and encouraging people who can help you stay motivated and focused.

Setbacks are not setbacks forever: It's essential to remember that a setback is not permanent. While it may feel like a significant blow in the moment, it is only temporary. Use this time to reflect, recharge, and regroup. Don't let it discourage you or make you give up on your goals.

Take action: Don't let setbacks and failures paralyze you. Instead, take action and address the issues at hand. Break down your goals into smaller, achievable tasks and work towards them. It can also be helpful to seek advice and guidance from mentors, friends, or professionals who can provide a fresh perspective and offer valuable insights.

Stay motivated: One of the most challenging aspects of overcoming setbacks and failures is maintaining motivation. Set realistic and achievable goals, and celebrate small victories along the way. Read success stories, watch motivational videos, or surround yourself with positive affirmations to keep your motivation levels high.

Setbacks and failures may seem like insurmountable obstacles, but they are a natural and necessary part of our journey towards success. Each one offers valuable lessons and opportunities for growth. By adopting a positive mindset, learning from mistakes, and practicing resilience, we can overcome setbacks and failures and emerge stronger and more resilient individuals. Remember to never give up on your dreams and keep pushing forward, no matter how many times you may stumble.

Strategies for dealing with failure

Failure is an inevitable part of life, and it is something that everyone experiences at some point in their lives. Whether it is in our personal or professional lives, failure can be a daunting and demoralizing experience. However, it is not the failure itself that defines us, but how we deal with it. In fact, many successful individuals and organizations attribute their achievements to the lessons learned from their failures. Therefore, it is important to develop effective strategies for dealing with failure. In this essay, we will discuss some strategies that can help individuals and organizations overcome and learn from failure.

Acknowledge and accept failure:
The first and most crucial step in dealing with failure is to acknowledge and accept it. Many people tend to deny or ignore their

failures, which only prolongs the negative impact it has on their lives. Accepting failure means acknowledging that it has happened and taking responsibility for it. This is not an easy step, but it is necessary for growth and improvement. It allows us to move on and focus on finding solutions.

Identify the cause of failure:
It is essential to determine the root cause of failure to prevent it from happening again. Was it because of a lack of effort, skills, resources, or external factors? Reflecting on what went wrong can provide valuable insights and help avoid making the same mistakes in the future.

Learn from failure:
Failure is an excellent teacher, and it provides an opportunity for us to learn and grow. Instead of dwelling on the negative aspects of failure, it is essential to look for the lessons it offers. What can we do differently? What skills do we need to acquire? How can we improve ourselves? By learning from our failures, we can become better equipped to handle future challenges.

Cultivate a positive mindset:

Having a positive mindset can make a significant difference in how we deal with failure. Instead of viewing it as a setback, see it as an opportunity to improve and try again. Embrace a growth mindset, where failure is seen as a part of the learning process rather than a reflection of our abilities or worth. This mindset allows us to bounce back stronger and more resilient after a failure.

Seek support:

Dealing with failure can be emotionally draining, and it is important to have a support system to lean on. Surround yourself with positive and supportive people who can provide encouragement and helpful advice. It is also helpful to talk to someone who has been through a similar experience and can offer valuable insights and guidance.

Set realistic goals:

Often, failures can occur because our goals are unrealistic or unattainable. It is crucial to set achievable goals and have a plan of action to reach them. By setting realistic goals, we can reduce the chances of failure and focus on making steady progress.

Persevere and be resilient:
Failure should not be seen as a roadblock, but rather as a detour. It is essential to persevere and be resilient during difficult times. Keep pushing forward, and use failure as motivation to keep moving towards your goals. Remember, success is not a linear path, and setbacks are a part of the journey.

Failure is inevitable, but it does not have to be a negative experience. By following these strategies, individuals and organizations can learn to embrace failure and use it as a stepping stone towards success. It is vital to remember that failure is not permanent, and with the right mindset and strategies, we can overcome and learn from it.

How to bounce back and persevere towards success

Life is unpredictable, and every one of us faces challenges and setbacks at some point in our journey towards success. It is not how many times we fall that matters, but how many times we rise and persevere towards our goals. Bouncing back from setbacks and difficulties is a crucial skill that can help us achieve success in all aspects of our lives. Here are some essential steps that one can follow to bounce back and persevere towards success.

Acknowledge and accept the setback:
The first step towards bouncing back is to recognize and accept the setback. Denial only prolongs the problem and hinders the recovery process. Understand that setbacks are a part of life, and it is okay to face them. By acknowledging the setback, we can stop dwelling on the negative thoughts and start finding solutions.

Stay positive:
A positive mindset is crucial in facing challenges and bouncing back from setbacks. Instead of focusing on the negative aspects, try to find the lessons and

opportunities that come with the setback. Cultivate a growth mindset, where you see challenges as a chance to learn and improve.

Reflect on the setback:
Take some time to reflect on the setback and try to find the reasons behind it. Was it something within your control, or was it an external factor? What lessons can you learn from this setback? By analyzing the situation, you can avoid making the same mistakes in the future and come up with a better plan to move forward.

Have a support system:
Having a support system of friends, family, or mentors can provide the necessary emotional and practical support during difficult times. Surround yourself with people who believe in you and encourage you to keep going. Talking to someone about your struggles can help you gain a new perspective and find solutions.

Keep your goals in mind:
In the face of setbacks, it is easy to lose sight of our goals and get discouraged. It is

essential to remind ourselves of the ultimate objective and the reasons why we started our journey towards success. Visualize your goals and use them as motivation to keep moving forward.

Take small steps:
When faced with a setback, it is natural to feel overwhelmed and unsure of the next step. Instead of trying to solve everything at once, break down the problem into smaller, more manageable steps. This will not only make the situation more manageable but also give you a sense of progress and achievement.

Be flexible:
Sometimes, our setbacks may require us to change our plans and adapt to a new situation. The ability to be flexible and open to change is crucial in bouncing back and persevering towards success. It is okay to alter our plans if it means getting closer to our goals.

Take care of yourself:
During challenging times, it is easy to neglect our physical and mental well-being.

However, taking care of ourselves is essential in bouncing back and maintaining the resilience needed to persevere towards success. Make sure to get enough rest, eat nutritious meals, and engage in activities that bring you joy and relaxation.

Learn from successful people:
Many successful individuals have faced setbacks and failures before achieving their goals. Reading about their stories and learning from their experiences can provide inspiration and valuable insights on how to bounce back and persevere towards success.

Never give up:
The most crucial step in bouncing back is to never give up. It may take time and effort, but with determination and perseverance, success is within reach. Keep pushing forward, and remember that setbacks do not define you; how you handle them does.

In conclusion, bouncing back from setbacks and persevering towards success is a journey that requires patience, determination, and a positive attitude. By following these steps and not letting setbacks hold us back, we can achieve our goals and lead a fulfilling and successful life.

Managing stress and handling pressure

Managing stress and handling pressure is an important aspect of maintaining mental and emotional well-being. Stress and pressure are inevitable aspects of life, but how we respond to them is crucial.

To effectively manage stress, it is important to identify the source of stress and develop healthy coping mechanisms. This can include practicing relaxation techniques, such as meditation or deep breathing, setting priorities and deadlines, and maintaining a balanced lifestyle with regular exercise and a healthy diet. It is also important to have a support system of friends and family to turn to for advice and emotional support.

Handling pressure involves developing resilience and the ability to adapt to changing circumstances. This can be achieved by setting realistic expectations for oneself and learning to effectively prioritize tasks. It also requires effective time management and problem-solving skills to meet deadlines and overcome challenges.

Seeking professional help, such as therapy or counseling, can also be useful in developing coping mechanisms and managing stress and pressure. Ultimately, it is important to recognize that stress and pressure are a normal part of life and finding ways to cope and manage them can lead to improved overall well-being.

Techniques for managing stress

Stress is an inevitable part of life, and learning how to manage it effectively is essential for overall health and well-being. When left unchecked, stress can lead to a variety of physical and mental health issues, including anxiety, depression, and heart disease. However, with the right techniques, it is possible to manage stress and reduce its negative effects. In this article, we will explore some effective techniques for managing stress.

Identify the source
The first step in managing stress is identifying its source. It could be work-related, relationship issues, financial problems, or health concerns. Take some time to reflect and understand what is causing your stress and what triggers it. Once you have identified the source, it will be easier to find specific strategies to manage it.

Practice relaxation techniques
Relaxation techniques can help to calm the mind and reduce stress levels. These include deep breathing, progressive muscle relaxation, guided imagery, and meditation. These techniques help to slow down the heart rate, lower blood pressure, and decrease muscle tension, promoting a sense of calmness and well-being.

Exercise regularly

Regular physical activity is an excellent way to manage stress. Exercise helps to release endorphins, also known as the "feel-good" hormones, which can improve mood and reduce stress levels. It also helps to relieve muscle tension and improve sleep, which can be affected by stress.

Get enough sleep

Lack of sleep can worsen feelings of stress. It is recommended to get at least seven to eight hours of quality sleep each night. Establishing a regular sleep routine, avoiding caffeine and electronics before bedtime, and creating a comfortable sleep environment can all help to improve sleep quality.

Practice time management

Many people feel stressed when they have too much to do and not enough time to do it. Learning to manage time effectively can help to reduce stress levels. Prioritizing tasks, delegating responsibilities, and setting boundaries can help to create a more balanced and manageable workload.

Seek advice

Talking to someone about your stress can be very beneficial. It can help to relieve pent-up emotions and provide a different perspective on the situation. Reach out to friends, family, or a therapist for support and guidance.

Make healthy lifestyle choices
Eating a healthy, well-balanced diet, and avoiding excessive alcohol and caffeine consumption can help to manage stress. These substances can worsen feelings of stress and anxiety. It is also essential to incorporate self-care activities such as reading, listening to music, or spending time in nature to promote relaxation and reduce stress.

In summary, managing stress is crucial for maintaining physical and mental health. With proper techniques, it is possible to reduce stress levels and promote a sense of well-being. It is essential to remember that what works for one person may not work for another, so it is crucial to find the right techniques that work for you. With consistency and patience, managing stress can become a manageable and less overwhelming task.

Coping mechanisms for handling pressure in high-stress situations

Coping mechanisms are strategies or techniques that individuals use to manage and deal with stress, particularly in high-pressure situations. These mechanisms are crucial for maintaining physical and mental well-being in times of immense stress and pressure. In order to effectively handle pressure in high-stress situations, it is important to understand and implement coping mechanisms that work best for each individual's unique needs.

Here are some common coping mechanisms that can help individuals handle pressure in high-stress situations:

Deep Breathing: Breathing exercises such as deep breathing can help to reduce stress and calm the mind. By focusing on slow and deep breaths, individuals can lower their heart rate and blood pressure, which can alleviate physical symptoms of stress.

Mindfulness: Mindfulness is the practice of being fully present and aware of one's thoughts, feelings, and surroundings. By focusing on the present moment, individuals can let go of worries about the past or future, and better cope with the stress in a particular situation.

Positive Self-Talk: In high-stress situations, negative thoughts and self-doubt can easily creep in. Positive self-talk, which involves replacing negative thoughts with positive and encouraging ones, can help individuals maintain a more optimistic outlook and handle pressure with more confidence.

Time Management: Feeling overwhelmed and under pressure often goes hand in hand with not having enough time to complete tasks or meet deadlines. Effective time management skills, such as prioritizing tasks and setting realistic goals, can help to reduce stress and increase productivity.

Seek Social Support: It is important to have a strong support system of friends, family, or colleagues who can offer a listening ear, provide words of encouragement, or even share their own experiences of handling high-stress situations. This can help individuals feel less alone and more capable of handling the pressure.

Physical Exercise: Regular physical exercise is not only beneficial for physical health but also for mental well-being. Engaging in any form of physical activity, whether it's a brisk walk or a yoga class, can help to release endorphins, which can improve mood and reduce stress levels.

Healthy Lifestyle Habits: Maintaining a healthy lifestyle is essential for managing stress. This includes getting enough sleep, eating a balanced diet, and limiting the consumption of alcohol, caffeine, and other stimulants. A healthy body can better handle stress and pressure.

Take Breaks: In high-stress situations, taking a break to step back and recharge can be beneficial. This could mean taking a short walk, listening to music, or engaging in a hobby. Taking breaks can help to reduce tension and increase focus when returning to the task at hand.

Cognitive Restructuring: This technique involves changing the way one thinks about a stressful situation. By reframing negative thoughts and focusing on the positive aspects, individuals can better cope with the pressure and find solutions to the problems they are facing.

Seek Professional Help: If the stress and pressure become too overwhelming, seeking professional help from a therapist or counselor can be beneficial. They can provide individuals with personalized coping strategies and techniques to help them manage high-stress situations effectively.

Coping mechanisms for handling pressure in high-stress situations are essential tools for maintaining physical and mental well-being. It is important for individuals to identify which coping mechanisms work best for them and to practice them regularly. By implementing these strategies, individuals can better manage their stress and handle pressure in a healthy and effective manner.

Chapter 7
Adaptability and Flexibility

Adaptability and flexibility are essential skills in today's fast-paced and ever-changing world. The ability to adapt to new situations and be flexible in one's approach can lead to success in both personal and professional life. Here are some reasons why adaptability and flexibility are important skills to possess:

Dealing with Change: In today's world, change is constant. Whether it is at the workplace, in personal life, or in society, things are constantly evolving. Those who are adaptable and flexible are better equipped to deal with change and are more likely to navigate through it successfully.

Problem-solving: Adaptability and flexibility require a creative and open-minded approach to problem-solving. When faced with a challenge, those with these skills can quickly come up with new and innovative solutions to overcome it.

Career Advancement: Employers highly value employees who are adaptable and flexible. These skills demonstrate an individual's ability to work under pressure, adjust to new situations, and take on new responsibilities. As a result, those who possess these skills are more likely to be considered for promotions and career advancement opportunities.

Resilience: The ability to adapt and be flexible helps individuals to become more resilient. They are better equipped to bounce back from setbacks and challenges, leading to a more positive and growth-oriented mindset.

Building Relationships: Adaptability and flexibility also play a crucial role in building and maintaining relationships. They allow individuals to be more understanding and accommodating of others, which can lead to stronger and more positive relationships.

Personal Growth: Constantly adapting and being open to change also leads to personal growth. Through new experiences and challenges, individuals learn more about themselves and their capabilities, which can help them grow and improve in all aspects of life.

Overall, being adaptable and flexible can lead to a more fulfilling and successful life. These skills are highly valued in both personal and professional settings and can set individuals apart from others. It is important to continuously work on developing and honing these skills to thrive and succeed in a constantly changing world.

Embracing change

Change is a part of life that we cannot escape. It is a constant force that shapes us and influences the world around us. Yet, many of us fear change and resist it, wanting to hold onto what is familiar and comfortable. However, embracing change can lead to personal growth, new opportunities and a more fulfilling life.

One of the most important reasons to embrace change is that it allows us to break out of our comfort zone. When we stay within our comfort zone, we limit ourselves and miss out on new experiences and opportunities. Embracing change means stepping into the unknown, which can be scary, but it also opens up a whole new world of possibilities. We may discover new interests, meet new people or find a new perspective on life.

Change also challenges us to adapt and be flexible. In today's fast-paced world, things are constantly changing, and those who are able to adapt quickly are the ones who thrive. Embracing change allows us to develop resilience and problem-solving skills, making us better equipped to handle any unexpected situations that may come our way.

Moreover, change often brings personal growth. When we resist change, we remain stagnant and do not allow ourselves to evolve. Embracing change means taking risks and trying new things, which can lead to personal development and self-discovery. We may discover strengths and abilities we never knew we had, and this can boost our confidence and self-esteem.

It is also important to remember that change is necessary for progress and development. Without embracing change, we would never grow as individuals or as a society. Just think about all the advancements and innovations that have been made throughout history because people were willing to embrace change. Whether it's in technology, medicine, or social movements, change is the driving force behind progress.

Embracing change also allows us to let go of the past and move forward. It can be difficult to leave behind what we are comfortable with, but clinging onto the past can hold us back from reaching our full potential. By embracing change, we learn to let go of what no longer serves us and move towards a brighter future.

To truly embrace change, we must also learn to let go of fear and trust in the process. Change can be unpredictable and scary, but it is important to have faith that everything will work out in the end. We may not always have control over the changes that happen in our lives, but we can control how we respond to them.

Change is an inevitable part of life, and by embracing it, we can open ourselves up to new experiences, personal growth and a more fulfilling life. So, instead of resisting change, let us choose to embrace it with open arms, confident in the knowledge that it will lead us to a better tomorrow.

Importance of being adaptable in a constantly changing world

In today's fast-paced and ever-evolving world, being adaptable is becoming increasingly important. With rapid advancements in technology, economic fluctuations, and unforeseen global events, individuals and organizations need to be able to quickly adjust and thrive in a constantly changing environment.

One of the key reasons why adaptability is crucial in today's world is because it allows individuals and organizations to stay relevant and competitive. Those who are able to quickly adapt to changing circumstances and embrace new ideas and technologies are more likely to succeed and thrive in their respective fields. For example, companies that were able to adapt their business strategies to the rise of e-commerce have seen tremendous growth and success, while those who resisted this change have struggled to keep up.

The ability to adapt also enables individuals and organizations to seize opportunities. In a rapidly changing world, new opportunities emerge constantly. Those who are adaptable and open to change are more likely to recognize and take advantage of these opportunities, leading to growth and success.

Furthermore, being adaptable also allows individuals and organizations to better manage risks and overcome challenges. In today's world, unexpected events such as natural disasters, economic downturns, and political upheavals can have a significant impact on businesses and individuals. Those who are adaptable are better equipped to face these challenges and find ways to overcome them, rather than being completely thrown off course.

In addition, adaptability helps individuals to cope with personal and professional changes. With shifting job markets and career paths, being adaptable allows individuals to embrace new opportunities and skills, making them more resilient in the face of change. It also allows individuals to adjust to new environments and cultures with ease, making them more open-minded and understanding.

Moreover, adaptability fosters innovation and creativity. Constantly changing environments require individuals and organizations to think outside the box and come up with new solutions to old problems. Being adaptable allows individuals to embrace change and harness their creativity to come up with novel ideas and approaches.

Overall, being adaptable is essential in a constantly changing world. It allows individuals and organizations to stay relevant, seize opportunities, manage risks and challenges, cope with personal and professional changes, and foster innovation. In order to thrive in today's world, it is crucial to cultivate the ability to adapt and embrace change. As the saying goes, "change is the only constant in life," and being adaptable is the key to not only surviving but thriving in a constantly changing world.

Ways to practice adaptability

Adaptability is the ability to adjust and thrive in different and changing situations. In today's world which is constantly evolving and full of uncertainties, being adaptable is a crucial skill to possess. Whether it's in our personal or professional lives, the ability to adapt can help us navigate challenges and achieve success. Here are some ways in which we can practice and improve our adaptability:

Be open to change: The first step towards practicing adaptability is to have an open mindset towards change. Instead of resisting it, try to embrace it as an opportunity for learning and growth. Understand that change is inevitable and can bring about positive outcomes.

Stay curious and keep learning: Being adaptable requires a willingness to learn new things and be open to new ideas. Cultivate a curious mindset and seek out new experiences and knowledge. This will not only help you adapt to new situations but also make you more versatile and valuable in any setting.

Embrace challenges: Challenges and setbacks are a part of life and can provide valuable lessons and opportunities for growth. Instead of shying away from them, view them as a chance to improve and sharpen your adaptability skills.

Practice resilience: The ability to bounce back from difficult situations is a key aspect of adaptability. Develop a resilient mindset by finding ways to cope with stress, setbacks, and failures. This will enable you to stay calm and focused even in the face of challenges.

Be open to feedback: Constructive feedback can improve our adaptability by helping us understand our strengths and weaknesses in different situations. Be open to receiving feedback and use it as a tool for self-improvement.

Emphasize flexibility: Being adaptable also means being flexible. Instead of sticking to rigid plans and routines, be open to adjusting them according to changing circumstances. This will help you adapt more easily to unexpected changes.

Practice problem-solving: When facing new situations, our ability to adapt depends on our problem-solving skills. Practice critical thinking and problem-solving techniques to help you overcome challenges and adjust to new environments.

Step out of your comfort zone: Adapting to new situations often requires stepping out of your comfort zone. Make a conscious effort to try new things and take on tasks that may be outside of your comfort zone. This will help you build resilience and broaden your adaptability skills.

Learn from others: Strive to surround yourself with people who possess strong adaptability skills. Observe and learn from them, and ask for their advice and insights. This will help you develop a more adaptable mindset and approach towards life.

Reflect and reassess: Take time to reflect on your experiences and adaptability skills. Be honest with yourself about areas that may need improvement and make a plan to work on them. Regularly reassessing your adaptability will help you continuously improve and evolve.

In conclusion, adaptability is a crucial skill that can help us thrive and succeed in a constantly changing world. By following these practices, we can improve and strengthen our ability to adapt and handle any situation that comes our way.

Being open to new ideas and perspectives

Being open to new ideas and perspectives is a crucial aspect of personal growth and development. It involves being receptive to different ways of thinking, challenging our own beliefs and biases, and embracing diversity in thoughts and opinions. It allows us to expand our knowledge, break out of our comfort zones, and gain a broader understanding of the world around us.

One of the key benefits of being open to new ideas and perspectives is the opportunity for intellectual stimulation. By welcoming new ideas, we invite different perspectives that can challenge our pre-existing beliefs and stimulate critical thinking. This can lead to expanding our knowledge base, challenging and refining our opinions, and fostering intellectual growth. It also helps to break us out of our own echo-chambers, where we are constantly surrounded by people who share the same ideas as us, limiting our growth potential.

One's willingness to consider new ideas and perspectives also promotes flexibility and adaptability. In this fast-paced and ever-evolving world, being able to adapt and think creatively is crucial for success. When we are open to new ideas, we are more likely to see things from different angles and find innovative solutions to problems. It also allows us to embrace change and uncertainty with an open mind, instead of being resistant and rigid in our thinking.

Being open to new ideas and perspectives can also help us to develop empathy and understanding towards others. By exposing ourselves to diverse viewpoints, we learn to see issues from different sides and build greater empathy towards others' experiences and struggles. This can cultivate a more tolerant and compassionate attitude towards people with different backgrounds, beliefs, and cultures. It also helps us to communicate and collaborate with people who may have different opinions and ideas, creating a more inclusive and harmonious environment.

Moreover, being open to new ideas and perspectives can enrich our personal and professional relationships. When we welcome diverse perspectives, we invite deeper and more meaningful conversations with others. This can lead to better communication, empathy, and a more open-minded dialogue between individuals. It also facilitates personal growth and development by exposing us to new experiences, opinions, and insights from those around us.

On a larger scale, being open to new ideas and perspectives can have a positive impact on society. By embracing diversity and being open-minded, we promote inclusivity, respect, and tolerance for all individuals, regardless of their beliefs and backgrounds. It also creates a more vibrant and diverse community where people can learn from each other and work towards a common goal.

Being open to new ideas and perspectives is essential for personal and societal growth. It allows us to expand our knowledge, foster critical thinking and creativity, and build empathy and understanding towards others. It is a continuous process that requires us to challenge our own beliefs, remain curious, and welcome diverse viewpoints. By being open to new ideas and perspectives, we can create a more dynamic, inclusive, and thriving world.

Benefits of being open-minded

Being open-minded means having a willingness to listen to and consider different ideas, perspectives, and beliefs without judgment or prejudice. It is the act of freeing our minds from the constraints of our own thoughts and opinions, and allowing new and diverse concepts to enter.
Open-mindedness is a valuable quality that

has a number of benefits in various aspects of our lives. In this essay, we will discuss some of the key benefits of being open-minded.

Expands Our Understanding: One of the primary benefits of being open-minded is that it broadens our understanding of the world. When we are open to listening to others and considering their perspectives, we gain a deeper understanding of different cultures, beliefs, and experiences. This, in turn, helps us to be more tolerant, empathetic, and accepting of others. We become more aware of the diverse ways of thinking and living, leading to a more inclusive and harmonious society.

Encourages Personal Growth: Being open-minded allows us to constantly learn and grow. When we are open to new ideas and perspectives, we are able to challenge our own beliefs and expand our knowledge. This ongoing process of learning and growth not only helps us to evolve as individuals, but it also enables us to adapt to changing situations, making us more resilient and successful in life.

Fosters Creativity and Innovation:
Open-mindedness is closely linked to creativity and innovation. When we are open to new ideas, we are more likely to think outside the box and come up with fresh and innovative solutions. This is because being open-minded allows us to see things from different angles and incorporate diverse perspectives, leading to greater creativity and innovation.

Improves Relationships:
Open-mindedness is a key ingredient in building and maintaining healthy relationships. When we are open to listening and understanding others, it creates a sense of trust and respect. This, in turn, leads to better communication, deeper connections, and stronger relationships. Open-mindedness also helps to prevent conflicts and misunderstandings, as we are more willing to compromise and find common ground with others.

Enhances Critical Thinking: Being open-minded helps us to think critically and analyze information from different perspectives. This allows us to see situations more objectively and make well-informed decisions. Additionally, open-mindedness enables us to evaluate our own beliefs and opinions, leading to personal growth and development. It also helps us to recognize and challenge prejudices and biases, leading to a more fair and just society.

Promotes Adaptability: In today's rapidly changing world, the ability to adapt is crucial. Being open-minded allows us to adapt and adjust to new situations, experiences, and challenges. By being open to new ideas and perspectives, we are able to break free from rigid thinking patterns and embrace change. This adaptability is a valuable skill that can help us navigate through life's ups and downs with resilience and positivity.

Open-mindedness has numerous benefits that contribute to our personal growth, relationships, and society as a whole. It expands our understanding, fosters creativity and innovation, improves relationships, enhances critical thinking, and promotes adaptability. By consciously practicing open-mindedness, we not only enrich our own lives but also create a more diverse, tolerant, and inclusive world. As the famous saying goes, "An open mind is a key to an open door."

Techniques for being more open to new ideas and perspectives

As human beings, we are naturally inclined to stick to what we know and are familiar with. We tend to have a certain set of beliefs, opinions and perspectives that we have developed over time and are comfortable with. However, in today's fast-paced and ever-changing world, being open to new ideas and perspectives is vital for personal growth and success.

Opening ourselves up to new ideas and perspectives is not always easy. It can be uncomfortable and even scary at times. However, it is a necessary step towards personal growth and development. By being open to new ideas and perspectives, we expand our knowledge and understanding of the world, challenge our preconceived notions, and become more well-rounded individuals.

So, how can we become more open to new ideas and perspectives? Here are some techniques that can help:

Practice active listening: Active listening involves fully concentrating on what the other person is saying without interrupting or judging. By actively listening, we can gain a better understanding of someone else's perspective and ideas. This can help broaden our own perspective and enable us to see things in a different light.

Engage in diverse experiences: Exposing ourselves to diverse experiences can open our minds to new ideas and perspectives. This can be as simple as trying out a new cuisine, visiting a new place, or attending a workshop on a topic we are not familiar with. These experiences help us break out of our comfort zone and see things from a different point of view.

Read and learn about different cultures:
Reading about different cultures and their customs and beliefs can broaden our understanding of the world and help us be more accepting of different perspectives. It can also give us insights into how other people live and think, leading to increased empathy and understanding.

Reflect on our own biases: We all have biases, whether conscious or unconscious. By reflecting on our own biases, we can identify and challenge them, allowing us to be more open to new ideas and perspectives.

Engage in respectful debates: Engaging in respectful debates with others who hold different opinions can help us see things from a different angle. It also allows us to challenge our own views and explore new ideas and perspectives.

Be curious: Curiosity is key to being open to new ideas and perspectives. When we are curious, we are more willing to explore and try new things without judgment. It also helps us ask questions, seek answers, and gain a deeper understanding of different ideas.

Practice empathy: Being empathetic means putting ourselves in someone else's shoes and trying to understand their perspective. By practicing empathy, we can break down barriers and be more receptive to new ideas and perspectives.

Be open-minded: Having an open mind means being willing to listen to and consider different ideas and perspectives, even if they differ from our own. It is important to remember that our way of thinking is not the only way, and being open-minded allows us to broaden our horizons and learn from others.

In conclusion, being open to new ideas and perspectives is a continuous process that requires effort and practice. It is essential to keep an open mind, engage in diverse experiences, and practice empathy and curiosity. By being open to new ideas and perspectives, we can continuously learn and grow, leading to personal growth and success in all aspects of life.

Problem-solving skills

Problem-solving skills are one of the most essential skill sets for success in both personal and professional life. It involves the ability to identify and understand a problem, analyze it, and come up with effective solutions. It is a systematic approach to overcome challenges and obstacles and reach a desired outcome.

In today's dynamic and ever-changing work environment, problem-solving skills are highly valued by employers. Whether you are working in a team or independently, problems are bound to arise, and having problem-solving skills can set you apart from the rest. It is a combination of critical thinking, creativity, and decision-making skills that enable individuals to find innovative solutions to complex problems.

One of the key aspects of problem-solving skills is the ability to identify the root cause of a problem. Many times, we tend to focus on the symptoms rather than the underlying issue. Identifying the core problem helps in finding the best possible solution. It involves asking the right questions, gathering information from various sources, and looking at the problem from different perspectives. This enables individuals to understand the problem better and come up with effective solutions.

Another important aspect of problem-solving skills is the ability to analyze the problem. This involves breaking down the problem into smaller, more manageable steps and evaluating the pros and cons of each possible solution. This step requires logical and critical thinking skills to assess the feasibility of different solutions. Effective problem solvers also possess the ability to think outside the box and come up with creative and innovative solutions.

Once the problem has been analyzed, the next step is to come up with a solution. This requires decision-making skills and the ability to take calculated risks. Effective problem solvers weigh the potential consequences of each solution and make a well-informed decision. They are not afraid to take risks and think outside the box to find the best possible solution.

Effective communication is also crucial in problem-solving. It involves conveying your ideas and thoughts clearly and concisely to others. This helps in getting the necessary buy-in and support from others for the proposed solution. Moreover, problems are often solved in a team setting, and effective communication helps in efficient collaboration and reaching a consensus.

Moreover, problem-solving skills also involve being proactive and taking the necessary steps to prevent problems from arising in the future. This requires a continuous improvement mindset, where individuals constantly look for ways to improve processes and procedures to avoid similar issues in the future.

Strategies for effective problem-solving

Problem-solving is an essential skill that is required in all aspects of life. It is the ability to identify and analyze problems, develop and implement effective solutions, and evaluate their success. Effective problem-solving not only helps in overcoming obstacles and challenges, but it also leads to personal and professional growth. In this article, we will discuss the strategies that can help you to solve problems effectively.

Identify the problem: The first step in problem-solving is to identify the problem. Take some time to define it clearly and understand what is causing it. This will help in developing an appropriate solution.

Gather information: Once you have identified the problem, gather all the necessary information related to it. This can be done by brainstorming, conducting research, or seeking input from others. Having a clear understanding of the problem will help in coming up with effective solutions.

Analyze the problem: Analyzing the problem involves breaking it down into smaller parts and identifying the root cause. This will help in understanding the complexity of the problem and coming up with a more targeted solution.

Think creatively: Problem-solving requires thinking outside the box. Be open to new ideas and approaches, and don't limit yourself to conventional thinking. This can help in finding unique and effective solutions.

Consider different perspectives: Sometimes, we get too invested in our own point of view, which can hinder our problem-solving process. It is essential to consider different perspectives and viewpoints, as this can provide valuable insights and help in finding a better solution.

Develop a plan of action: Once you have gathered all the necessary information and analyzed the problem, it is time to develop a plan of action. This should include a clear and detailed outline of the steps that need to be taken to solve the problem.

Implement the solution: Put your plan into action and start working towards solving the problem. Be flexible and open to making changes if needed. Keep track of your progress and make adjustments as necessary.

Evaluate the solution: Once the solution has been implemented, it is critical to evaluate its effectiveness. Did it solve the problem? Is there room for improvement? Take note of what worked and what didn't, as this can be useful for future problem-solving efforts.

Learn from failures: Not all solutions will work, and that's okay. It is essential to learn from failures and use them as opportunities for growth. Analyze what went wrong and how it can be avoided in the future.

Practice problem-solving: The more you practice problem-solving, the better you will become at it. Look for opportunities to solve problems in your personal and professional life. This will help in sharpening your skills and making you a more effective problem solver.

In conclusion, effective problem-solving is a combination of critical thinking, creativity, and perseverance. By following these strategies, you can tackle any problem that comes your way with confidence and efficiency. Remember to stay calm and focused, be open to new ideas, and always be willing to learn from your experiences. With practice, you will become a skilled problem solver, making you an invaluable asset in any setting.

How to approach and overcome challenging situations

Approaching and dealing with challenging situations is something that we all experience at one point or another in our lives. Whether it is a difficult task, a personal problem, or a crisis, these situations can often leave us feeling overwhelmed, anxious, and incapable. However, it is essential to remember that challenges are a part of life, and it is how we approach and overcome them that defines us. With the right mindset and strategies, anyone can learn how to deal with challenging situations effectively. Here are some tips to help you approach and overcome challenging situations with confidence and resilience.

Accept the Situation

The first step to dealing with any challenging situation is to accept it for what it is. Denying or avoiding the issue will only make it more difficult to overcome. Acknowledge the problem or challenge and understand that it is a natural part of life. Avoiding it or pretending it doesn't exist will only increase your stress and anxiety.

Stay Positive

Maintaining a positive mindset is crucial when it comes to handling challenges. Instead of dwelling on the negative aspects of the situation, focus on the positive. Remind yourself of your past successes and the difficult situations you have overcome before. Positive self-talk and a can-do attitude can go a long way in giving you the motivation and confidence to face the challenge.

Analyze the Situation

Once you have accepted the situation and have a positive mindset, it is time to analyze the problem at hand. Break down the challenge into smaller, more manageable tasks. This will help you gain a better understanding of the situation and make it less daunting. Analyzing the situation will also help you identify the root cause of the problem, which can help in finding an effective solution.

Ask for Help

It is okay to ask for help when facing a challenging situation. Seeking support from friends, family, or even a professional can provide you with a fresh perspective, advice, or guidance. Sometimes, talking to someone can help you see the situation in a new light and come up with a solution that you may not have thought of before.

Develop a Plan

Now that you have a better understanding of the situation and have sought help if needed, it is time to develop a plan of action. List down the steps that you need to take to overcome the challenge and prioritize them according to their urgency and importance. Having a plan will not only give you a sense of control, but it will also help you stay focused and motivated.

Be Flexible

While having a plan is crucial, it is also essential to be flexible. You may face unexpected roadblocks or challenges along the way, and it is crucial to adapt and modify your plan accordingly. Being open to change and improvisation will increase your chances of success and make the process less stressful.

Practice Self-Care

Dealing with challenging situations can be mentally and emotionally draining. It is crucial to take care of yourself during this time. Make sure to get enough rest, eat well, and engage in activities that bring you joy and relaxation. Taking care of your physical and mental well-being will help you maintain a positive attitude and handle the situation better.

Learn from the Experience

Finally, remember that every challenging situation is an opportunity to learn and grow. Reflect on how you dealt with the situation and think about what you could have done differently. This will not only help you overcome the current challenge, but it will also prepare you to face similar situations in the future.

Chapter 8
Self-discipline and Accountability

Self-discipline and accountability are two important aspects of personal growth and development. They require individuals to take responsibility for their actions, make conscious choices, and stay committed to their goals and values.

Self-discipline can be defined as the ability to control one's behavior and actions in order to achieve desired outcomes. It involves making consistent effort and persevering through challenges, even when one is tempted to give in to distractions or temptations. Self-discipline is not something that comes naturally to everyone; it requires practice and determination to cultivate. However, it is a crucial trait to possess as it helps individuals to be more focused, productive, and successful in their endeavors.

Accountability, on the other hand, is the willingness to take responsibility for one's actions and decisions. It is the recognition that one's choices have consequences and being ready to face them. Accountability involves being honest with oneself and others, admitting mistakes, and taking necessary steps to rectify them. It is a sign of maturity and self-awareness, and it helps individuals to learn from their experiences and grow as individuals.

Together, self-discipline and accountability create a powerful combination that can lead to personal growth and success. When an individual has a strong sense of self-discipline, they are more likely to make responsible decisions and take ownership of their actions. Similarly, when one holds themselves accountable for their choices, they are more motivated to stay disciplined and focused on their goals because they understand the impact of their actions.

One of the main benefits of self-discipline and accountability is the development of good habits. By consistently practicing self-discipline and being accountable for their actions, individuals can form positive habits such as time management, goal setting, and self-care. These habits can lead to increased productivity, improved relationships, and a better overall quality of life.

Moreover, self-discipline and accountability also foster a sense of control and independence. When individuals are disciplined, they are less likely to rely on external factors to make decisions for them.

They take charge of their own lives and are empowered to make choices that align with their values and goals. Additionally, being accountable means being in control of one's outcomes rather than blaming external factors for failures or mistakes.

In contrast, the lack of self-discipline and accountability can lead to negative consequences such as procrastination, poor health choices, and strained relationships. When individuals are not disciplined, they may struggle to achieve their goals and may constantly feel stressed and overwhelmed. Similarly, the lack of accountability can result in a lack of trust and damaged relationships, both personally and professionally.

Understanding self-discipline

Self-discipline is having the ability to control your thoughts, actions, and emotions in order to achieve a goal or maintain a certain behavior. It involves restraining oneself from giving in to short-term gratification or impulses in order to focus on long-term goals and values.

Self-discipline requires a level of self-awareness, willpower, and determination. It means being able to prioritize and stick to a plan, even when faced with distractions, temptations, or difficulties.

Having self-discipline can lead to personal and professional success by helping individuals stay motivated and productive, as well as developing positive habits and a sense of self-control.

However, self-discipline is not the same as being strict or harsh on oneself. It is about being self-aware and making conscious choices that align with one's goals and values. It also involves being kind and forgiving towards oneself when faced with setbacks or mistakes.

Overall, self-discipline is an important skill to cultivate in order to live a purposeful and fulfilled life. It requires consistent effort and practice, but the benefits can greatly impact one's well-being and success.

Definition and importance of self-discipline

Self-discipline is the ability to control one's thoughts, actions, and emotions in order to achieve a certain goal or maintain a certain standard. It is a fundamental aspect of self-control and is essential for personal growth and development. Self-discipline involves setting aside impulses and desires in order to make rational and logical decisions. It requires one to prioritize their long-term goals and values over short-term gratification. In other words, self-discipline is about taking charge of one's own life and being in control of one's own choices.

One of the great philosophers, Aristotle, defined self-discipline as a mean between two extremes – excess and deficiency. He believed that self-discipline is the key to achieving a state of balance and harmony in one's life. This means avoiding extremes of indulgence and deprivation, and instead finding the right balance that leads to a fulfilling and successful life.

Self-discipline is a crucial aspect of personal development as it helps individuals to develop a strong sense of self-control and willpower. This is crucial for achieving success in all aspects of life, including career, relationships, and personal growth. Without self-discipline, it is easy to fall into bad habits and give in to temptations. As a result, one may struggle to achieve their goals and maintain healthy relationships with others.

Furthermore, self-discipline is essential for building self-esteem and self-confidence. When one is disciplined, they are more likely to achieve their goals and experience a sense of accomplishment. This, in turn, boosts self-esteem and encourages individuals to take on new challenges and strive for personal growth. With self-discipline, one becomes more self-reliant and confident in their abilities, making them less dependent on external validation.

In addition, self-discipline plays a crucial role in maintaining good physical and mental health. It requires individuals to make healthy choices and avoid harmful behaviors. This includes sticking to a healthy diet, exercising regularly, and avoiding addictive substances. By practicing self-discipline, individuals can maintain a healthy body and mind, which is essential for leading a fulfilling and happy life.

Moreover, self-discipline is also important for building strong and meaningful relationships. A disciplined individual is more likely to be reliable, responsible, and trustworthy. They are able to control their emotions and reactions, which helps them to communicate effectively and handle conflicts in a calm and mature manner. This, in turn, leads to stronger and more harmonious relationships with others.

The lack of self-discipline can have many negative consequences, including procrastination, poor time management, and low self-esteem. It can also lead to addictions, unhealthy relationships, and a general lack of direction in life. However, with self-discipline, individuals can overcome these challenges and lead a more fulfilling and successful life.

Self-discipline is crucial for personal growth and development. It allows individuals to take control of their lives and make positive choices that align with their values and goals. By practicing self-discipline, individuals can achieve success in all areas of life, including relationships, career, and personal growth. It is a lifelong journey that requires commitment and determination, but the benefits of self-discipline are far-reaching and essential for living a purposeful and fulfilling life.

Tips for developing self-discipline

Self-discipline is the ability to control one's own behavior, emotions, and thoughts in the pursuit of a goal or a set of values. It is a crucial skill that enables individuals to overcome procrastination, distractions, and temptations in order to achieve success. Developing self-discipline takes time and effort, but it is a valuable investment that can lead to a more fulfilling and productive life. Here are some tips for developing self-discipline:

Set clear and achievable goals: Having a clear idea of what you want to achieve is the first step in developing self-discipline. Set realistic and specific goals and write them down. This will help you stay focused and motivated.

Create a plan: Once you have set your goals, make a plan on how to achieve them. Break down your goals into smaller, manageable steps. This will give you a sense of direction and make it easier to stay on track.

Practice self-awareness: Pay attention to your thoughts, emotions, and behaviors. Identify the obstacles that are preventing you from achieving your goals. This self-awareness will help you understand the areas where you need to improve.

Start small: If you are used to giving in to instant gratification, it can be challenging to develop self-discipline overnight. Start with small tasks and gradually increase the difficulty. This will help you build your self-control muscles and make it easier to tackle bigger challenges.

Stay committed: Developing self-discipline requires commitment and consistency. It is essential to stay focused and determined even when faced with setbacks. Remind yourself of your goals and the reasons why you are working towards them.

Practice delayed gratification: Self-discipline is all about delaying gratification. Instead of giving in to your impulses, learn to postpone immediate pleasure for greater rewards in the future. This will help you develop a long-term perspective and make better decisions.

Eliminate distractions: Distractions can derail your progress and make it hard to stay disciplined. Identify the things that distract you and find ways to eliminate or minimize them. This could mean turning off your phone or avoiding certain websites while you are working.

Reward yourself: Celebrating small wins can boost your motivation and help you stay disciplined. Set up a reward system for yourself whenever you achieve a milestone. However, make sure your rewards support your goals rather than hinder them.

Surround yourself with like-minded people: The people you surround yourself with can have a significant impact on your level of discipline. Surround yourself with people who share similar goals and values. They can provide support and accountability to help you stay disciplined.

Be kind to yourself: Developing self-discipline is not easy, and there will be times when you slip up. It is crucial to be kind to yourself and practice self-compassion. Rather than beating yourself up over a mistake, acknowledge it, learn from it, and move on.

Developing self-discipline is a continuous process that requires patience, perseverance, and determination. It is about making intentional choices that align with your goals and values. By following these tips, you can start building your self-discipline and achieve success in all areas of your life.

Holding oneself accountable

Holding oneself accountable is an important and necessary characteristic for personal and professional growth. It refers to taking full responsibility for one's actions, decisions, and behavior, and facing the consequences that come with them. In other words, it means owning up to one's mistakes, admitting faults, and striving to improve oneself.

When an individual holds themselves accountable, they not only take full responsibility for their actions but also acknowledge the impact of their actions on others. This allows them to understand the consequences of their behavior and make amends for any harm caused. It also helps in building trust, respect, and credibility in relationships, both personal and professional.

One of the main benefits of holding oneself accountable is personal growth. When an individual takes ownership of their actions and decisions, they are more likely to reflect on their behavior, identify areas of improvement, and take necessary steps to change and grow. This leads to a better understanding of oneself and the ability to make better choices in the future.

Holding oneself accountable also fosters a sense of discipline and self-discipline. It requires an individual to be self-aware and self-motivated to adhere to their commitments and follow through with their responsibilities. This helps in building a strong work ethic and a sense of discipline that can positively impact other aspects of one's life.

In a professional setting, holding oneself accountable is crucial for success. It allows individuals to take ownership of their work, meet deadlines, and deliver quality results. This not only reflects positively on their work ethic but also contributes to the overall success of the team and the organization.

In contrast, individuals who do not hold themselves accountable tend to shift blame, make excuses, and avoid taking responsibility for their actions. This not only hinders their personal growth but also affects the trust and credibility in their relationships.

To hold oneself accountable, one must possess a strong sense of self-awareness. This entails being honest with oneself, acknowledging strengths and weaknesses, and actively working towards improvement. Additionally, setting clear and achievable goals and regularly evaluating progress can help in tracking one's accountability.

It is also essential to have a growth mindset. This means viewing mistakes and failures as opportunities for learning and growth, rather than weaknesses or setbacks. With a growth mindset, an individual becomes more resilient, adaptable, and accountable for their actions.

Generally, holding oneself accountable is a critical aspect of personal and professional development. It requires individuals to take responsibility for their actions, strive for improvement, and maintain a growth mindset. Cultivating this quality can lead to personal growth, build strong relationships, and contribute to success in various aspects of life.

Why accountability is important for success

Accountability is define
d as the obligation to accept responsibility for one's actions or decisions. In other words, being accountable means taking ownership of one's choices and their consequences. It is an essential aspect of success in both personal and professional spheres. The concept of accountability is often associated with integrity and trustworthiness, and it plays a crucial role in maintaining a healthy and productive society. In this essay, we will explore why accountability is crucial for success and how

it contributes to personal and professional growth.

First and foremost, accountability is important for success because it helps individuals stay true to their goals and commitments. When one is accountable, they are more likely to follow through with their promises and fulfill their responsibilities. This is essential for achieving success as it requires discipline and perseverance, which can only be maintained through being accountable. Moreover, being accountable also instills a sense of reliability and trustworthiness in an individual, which is highly valued in all aspects of life, whether it is personal relationships or professional endeavors.

In the workplace, accountability is vital for the success of both the individual and the organization. In order to achieve goals and meet deadlines, every team member must take responsibility for their actions and be accountable for their tasks. This not only ensures the effective completion of the project but also fosters a sense of ownership and commitment among employees. In a highly competitive and fast-paced work environment, having a sense of accountability can make a significant difference in the success of an organization.

Accountability also plays a crucial role in personal growth and development. Accepting responsibility for one's actions allows for self-reflection and learning from mistakes. When an individual takes ownership of their choices and decisions, they are more likely to reflect on their actions and make necessary changes to improve themselves. This leads to personal growth and development, which is a key factor in achieving success in various aspects of life. It also helps individuals to develop a strong sense of self-awareness and integrity, which are essential qualities in a successful person.

Furthermore, accountability also contributes to a positive and healthy work culture. In a team, when each member is held accountable for their actions, it promotes a sense of fairness and equality. This leads to open communication and a mutual understanding of expectations, which in turn fosters a positive and supportive work environment. When team members are accountable, they are also more likely to take ownership of problems and work together to find solutions. This not only leads to increased productivity but also strengthens the team dynamic, which is crucial for the success of any project or organization.

Additionally, accountability is important for success because it promotes a sense of transparency and reduces the likelihood of unethical practices. In both personal and professional contexts, being accountable means being honest and taking responsibility for one's actions. This is important in maintaining trust and credibility, not only with others but also with oneself. When one is accountable, it also helps to uphold ethical standards and promotes a culture of honesty and integrity.

Accountability is a crucial component of success in both personal and professional aspects of life. It not only helps individuals achieve their goals and fulfill their responsibilities, but also contributes to personal growth, fosters a positive work culture, and upholds ethical values. Without accountability, it is difficult to achieve success as it requires a strong sense of responsibility and commitment. Therefore, it is essential for individuals to understand the importance of accountability and make it a priority in their lives to achieve their desired level of success.

Ways to hold yourself accountable

Holding yourself accountable is a crucial aspect of personal growth and success. It involves taking responsibility for your actions, acknowledging your mistakes, and learning from them. Holding yourself accountable can be challenging, but it is necessary for self-improvement and achieving your goals. In this article, we will discuss some effective ways to hold yourself accountable.

Set clear and specific goals: The first step in holding yourself accountable is to have a clear understanding of what you want to achieve. Most people fail to accomplish their goals because they are not specific enough. When setting goals, make sure they are achievable, measurable, and time-bound. This will help you stay focused and track your progress, making it easier to hold yourself accountable.

Write it down: Writing down your goals and plans is a powerful way to hold yourself accountable. It adds a sense of commitment and makes your intentions more tangible. Write down not only your goals but also the steps you will take to achieve them. This will serve as a constant reminder of what you need to do and help you stay on track.

Create a schedule: Time management plays a significant role in holding yourself accountable. Without a proper schedule, it is easy to get sidetracked and lose focus. Set a daily, weekly, or monthly schedule, depending on your goals and tasks. Make sure to allocate time for each task and stick to the schedule to ensure that you are making progress towards your goals.

Find an accountability partner: Having someone to hold you accountable can make a big difference in achieving your goals. This can be a friend, family member, mentor, or even a professional coach. Share your goals and plans with them and ask them to check in with you regularly to see your progress. Their encouragement, support, and constructive feedback can help keep you motivated and remind you of your commitment to yourself.

Monitor your progress: It is essential to regularly monitor your progress towards your goals. This will give you an idea of how far you have come and what steps you need to take next. You can use various methods to track your progress, such as journaling, creating a progress chart, or using a productivity app. This will not only help you hold yourself accountable but also give you a sense of accomplishment when you see how much you have achieved.

Be honest with yourself: Holding yourself accountable requires honesty. It is essential to be honest with yourself about your strengths, weaknesses, and progress.

Acknowledge when you have made a mistake or fallen short of your goals. This will help you learn from your mistakes and make necessary adjustments to stay on track. Being honest with yourself also means taking responsibility for your actions and not making excuses or blaming others.

Reward yourself: Celebrating your accomplishments, no matter how small, is an essential part of holding yourself accountable. When you reach a milestone or complete a task, reward yourself in some way. This could be treating yourself to something you enjoy, taking a break, or simply acknowledging your hard work. Rewarding yourself will help you stay motivated and reinforce your commitment to achieving your goals.

Holding yourself accountable is a continuous process that requires discipline, self-awareness, and a strong desire for self-improvement. By setting clear goals, creating a schedule, finding an accountability partner, monitoring your progress, being honest with yourself, and rewarding yourself, you can effectively hold yourself accountable and achieve your goals. Remember, the key to success is taking responsibility for your actions and continuously striving to become the best version of yourself.

Avoiding procrastination

Procrastination is the act of delaying or putting off tasks and responsibilities that need to be done. It is a common behavior that affects people of all ages and can have detrimental effects on one's personal and professional life. While procrastination may seem harmless at first, it can lead to increased stress levels, missed deadlines, and a decrease in productivity. Therefore, it is crucial to learn how to avoid procrastination and improve our overall efficiency.

Recognize the problem
The first step to overcoming procrastination is to acknowledge that there is a problem. People often procrastinate because they have a fear of failure or a lack of motivation.

They may also struggle with time management skills, have perfectionistic tendencies, or find certain tasks too overwhelming. It is essential to identify the underlying causes of procrastination to find effective solutions.

Set clear goals and prioritize

Having a clear goal in mind can act as a powerful motivator to get things done. When setting goals, it is crucial to make them specific, measurable, achievable, realistic, and time-bound (SMART). This allows us to break down the task into smaller, manageable steps and prioritize what needs to be done first. With a structured plan in place, it becomes easier to overcome the desire to procrastinate.

Eliminate distractions

In today's digital age, distractions are everywhere, making it challenging to stay focused on a task. To avoid procrastination, it is essential to minimize distractions as much as possible. This may include turning off notifications on your phone, finding a quiet workspace, or using productivity tools such as website blockers. By removing potential distractions, we can create a more conducive environment for completing tasks.

Break tasks into smaller chunks
Large and overwhelming tasks can often lead to procrastination. Instead of trying to tackle the task all at once, break it down into smaller, more manageable chunks. This can help reduce the feeling of being overwhelmed and make it easier to get started. Furthermore, completing smaller tasks gives a sense of accomplishment, providing the motivation to keep going.

Create a schedule and stick to it
Working without a plan can lead to aimless wandering and procrastination. To avoid this, it is crucial to create a daily or weekly schedule and stick to it. Schedule time for each task, including breaks, and make sure to hold yourself accountable for following through. This can also help in prioritizing tasks and avoiding last-minute rush jobs. It is also essential to allocate extra time for unexpected tasks or delays.

Use positive self-talk

Procrastination is often fueled by negative self-talk and thoughts of failure. To combat this, it is vital to practice positive self-talk. Instead of saying, "I can't do this," tell yourself, "I will give my best effort." This can help overcome fear and build confidence. Additionally, celebrating small achievements and rewarding yourself after completing a task can help boost motivation and encourage productive behavior.

Find an accountability partner or support group

Having someone who can hold us accountable for our actions can be a powerful tool in avoiding procrastination. This could be a friend, family member, or even a colleague. Share your goals and schedule with them and ask them to check in on your progress regularly. Joining a support group with individuals who struggle with procrastination can also provide a sense of community and motivation to overcome this habit.

Seek help

For some individuals, procrastination can be a symptom of underlying mental health issues such as anxiety or depression. In such cases, seeking professional help may be necessary. Therapy or counseling can provide tools and strategies to manage procrastination and address any underlying issues contributing to it.

Avoiding procrastination requires self-awareness, motivation, and discipline. By setting clear goals, managing time effectively, and minimizing distractions, we can overcome the urge to put off tasks and become more productive. Remember to be patient and kind to yourself, as overcoming procrastination is a gradual process. With consistent effort and the right strategies, we can break free from the habit of procrastination and achieve our goals.

effects of procrastination

Procrastination, or the act of putting off tasks that need to be done, is a common problem that affects many people. While it may provide temporary relief and a sense of avoiding stress, it can have several negative effects in the long run. In this essay, we will discuss some of the major negative effects of procrastination.

One of the most significant negative effects of procrastination is the increase in stress and anxiety. When we procrastinate, we tend to avoid dealing with our responsibilities until the last minute. This can lead to a buildup of stress as deadlines loom closer and the pressure to complete the task increases. The constant worry and guilt about not being able to complete the task on time can also lead to anxiety and affect our mental health.

Another negative effect of procrastination is a decrease in productivity. When we put off important tasks, we end up wasting precious time that could have been used to complete them. This can lead to a decrease in productivity and efficiency, as we often rush to complete the tasks at the last minute. Furthermore, procrastination often leads to poor quality work, as we do not have enough time to give our best effort.

Procrastination can also have a negative impact on our personal and professional relationships. When we constantly postpone tasks and don't meet deadlines, it can be perceived as a lack of responsibility and reliability. This can harm our relationships with colleagues, friends, and family as they may start to view us as unreliable or careless.

Furthermore, procrastination can have serious consequences in our academic or professional lives. In academic settings, consistently putting off studying or completing assignments can result in poor grades and even failure in important exams. In the workplace, procrastination can lead to missed deadlines, unfinished projects, and even job loss. These consequences can have a significant impact on our future opportunities and goals.

Apart from these external effects, procrastination can also have a profound impact on our internal motivation and self-esteem. When we continuously procrastinate and fail to complete tasks, we start to doubt our ability to accomplish goals. This can lead to a decrease in self-confidence and motivation, making it harder to be productive and achieve our goals in the future.

Techniques for overcoming procrastination and staying focused

Procrastination and lack of focus are common obstacles that often hinder our progress and productivity. They can lead to missed deadlines, unfinished projects, and added stress and anxiety. Overcoming these habits is crucial for achieving our goals and feeling a sense of accomplishment. Here are some effective techniques for overcoming procrastination and staying focused.

Set clear and realistic goals
Having a clear understanding of what you want to achieve can help you stay focused and motivated. Set specific, achievable, and time-bound goals for yourself. This will help you break down your tasks into smaller,

manageable chunks and prevent you from feeling overwhelmed.

Create a schedule or to-do list

Creating a schedule or a to-do list can help you stay organized and on track. Prioritize your tasks based on their importance and deadlines, and try to tackle the most challenging ones first. You can use a planner or a productivity app to keep track of your tasks and progress.

Identify and eliminate distractions

Distractions are one of the biggest sources of procrastination and lack of focus. Identify what distracts you the most, whether it's your phone, social media, or a noisy environment, and find ways to eliminate or minimize these distractions. This could mean turning off your phone, working in a quiet place, or using website blockers to limit your time on social media.

Practice the Pomodoro technique

The Pomodoro technique is a time-management method that involves breaking your work into intervals, usually 25 minutes, separated by short breaks. This can help you work more efficiently and stay focused, as you know you have a set amount of time to complete a task. After four pomodoros, take a longer break of 15-20 minutes.

Use the "5-second rule"
The 5-second rule, popularized by Mel Robbins, involves counting down from 5 to 1 and taking immediate action on a task. This technique is based on the idea that our mind will try to talk us out of doing things that are uncomfortable or require effort, and counting down helps us to override this initial resistance.

Break down large tasks into smaller ones
Sometimes, the thought of a large and overwhelming task can lead to procrastination. In such cases, breaking down the task into smaller, more manageable ones can make it seem less daunting and more achievable. This can also give you a sense of progress as you complete each task, keeping you motivated and focused.

Practice mindfulness and meditation

Mindfulness and meditation can help you become more aware of your thoughts and emotions. By practicing mindfulness, you can catch yourself in moments of procrastination and gently redirect your attention back to your work. You can also use a meditation session to clear your mind and increase your focus before starting a task.

Take breaks and reward yourself

Working for long periods without breaks can lead to burnout and decreased productivity. It's essential to take regular breaks to recharge your mind and body. You can also use breaks as incentives and rewards for completing tasks. For example, you can take a short walk or listen to your favorite music after completing a task.

Visualize the end result

Visualizing the end result of your work can help you stay motivated and focused. Imagine how you will feel once you have completed the task or achieved your goal. Use this image as a source of inspiration and motivation to keep you going.

Seek accountability and support

Sometimes, having someone else hold us accountable can be a powerful motivator. Find an accountability partner, whether it's a friend, family member, or colleague, and share your goals and progress with them. Knowing that someone else is counting on you can push you to stay focused and avoid procrastination. Additionally, seeking support from friends and family can provide you with encouragement and motivation when you need it.

Overcoming procrastination and staying focused is essential for achieving our goals and reaching our full potential. It may take some time and effort, but by implementing these techniques and finding what works best for you, you can overcome these habits and become more productive and successful. Remember, every small step counts, and with consistency and determination, you can overcome any obstacle.

Chapter 9
Financial Management

Financial Management is a crucial subject that helps ensure optimum utilization of resources in a business and maximizes the returns on investment for the company's stakeholders. It involves planning, organizing, controlling, and monitoring financial resources to achieve the company's objectives.

Good financial management involves making decisions that will have a positive impact on the company's financial health, such as budgeting, cash flow management, and investment strategies. It also involves identifying potential risks and taking necessary steps to mitigate them.

The primary goal of financial management is to increase the value of the business by generating higher profits and managing risks effectively. It also provides insights into the company's financial position, which helps in making informed decisions and analyzing the company's performance.

One of the essential components of financial management is budgeting. Budgeting is the process of setting financial goals and creating a plan to achieve them. It helps in allocating resources, monitoring expenses, and ensuring that the company operates within its financial capability. A well-planned budget also helps in forecasting future financial needs and identifying potential areas for cost-cutting.

Financial management also includes effective cash flow management. Cash flow refers the movement of cash in and out of a business. It is essential to have a positive cash flow to cover day-to-day expenses and keep the business running smoothly. Effective cash flow management involves monitoring cash inflows and outflows, analyzing trends, and taking necessary actions to manage any fluctuations.

Investment strategies play a crucial role in financial management. A company's investments should align with its financial goals and risk appetite. It involves making informed decisions about which assets to invest in, how much to invest, and for how long. A diverse investment portfolio helps in reducing risks and increasing potential returns.

Another crucial aspect of financial management is managing risk. Every business faces various risks, including market risk, credit risk, operational risk, and liquidity risk. Effective risk management involves identifying potential risks, analyzing their impact, and taking necessary steps to mitigate them. It also involves having contingency plans in place to address any unforeseen events or emergencies.

Financial management also includes financial reporting and analysis. Financial reports provide a detailed overview of the company's financial performance, including its assets, liabilities, income, and expenses. These reports help in identifying areas for improvement and making informed decisions.

In today's business landscape, technology plays a crucial role in financial management. Various software solutions and tools are available to automate financial processes, improve efficiency, and reduce the risk of human error.

Overall, financial management is a crucial aspect of every business. It involves planning, organizing, controlling, and monitoring financial resources to achieve the company's objectives. Effective financial management helps in maximizing profits, minimizing risks, and ensuring the company's long-term success. It requires a deep understanding of financial principles, strong analytical skills, and the ability to make informed decisions based on data. With proper financial management, companies can thrive and achieve their goals in a dynamic and competitive market.

Importance of financial management

Financial management is an essential aspect of running a successful organization. It involves the planning, organizing, monitoring, and controlling of an organization's financial resources. It is crucial for the efficient and effective utilization of funds, which ultimately leads to the achievement of the organization's goals and objectives. Financial management ensures that all the financial resources of an organization are managed in a way that maximizes profits and minimizes risks.

The following are the key reasons why financial management is important for an organization:

Facilitates decision-making: Effective financial management enables an organization to make informed and strategic decisions. It provides a comprehensive analysis of the company's financial position, which helps the management to evaluate the profitability and financial stability of the organization. This, in turn, guides them in making decisions related to investments, expansion, and cost-cutting measures.

Helps in resource allocation: Financial management plays a vital role in allocating resources appropriately. It helps in determining the allocation of resources to various departments, projects, or investments, depending on their potential for generating returns. This ensures that resources are utilized efficiently and effectively, which, in turn, leads to the organization's growth and success.

Ensures adequate funding: For an organization to thrive, it needs a continuous flow of funds from various sources like investors, banks, or profits. Financial management is crucial in maintaining adequate funding to meet the company's financial obligations, such as paying salaries, purchasing raw materials, and investing in research and development. Without proper financial management, the organization may run into financial difficulties, which can affect its operations and reputation.

Controls costs and increases efficiency: Effective financial management helps in controlling costs and increasing efficiency. With proper financial planning and budgeting, an organization can track its expenses and identify areas where costs can be reduced. This, in turn, leads to increased efficiency and profitability. Moreover, financial management helps in achieving economies of scale, leading to lower production costs and higher profits.

Assists in risk management: Every business faces risks, and effective financial management helps in identifying, mitigating, and managing these risks. Proper financial planning and forecasting enable the organization to anticipate potential financial risks and take necessary measures to minimize their impact. It also helps in developing contingency plans to deal with uncertain situations, such as economic downturns, natural disasters, or unplanned expenses.

Enhances investment opportunities: With sound financial management, an organization can attract more investors and secure funding for expansion and growth opportunities. Investors are more likely to invest in an organization that has a strong financial track record and efficient management of funds. This enables the organization to expand its operations, enter new markets, and develop new products, which ultimately leads to increased profitability.

Promotes transparency and accountability: Financial management involves maintaining accurate financial records and preparing reliable financial statements. This promotes transparency and accountability within the organization, which is crucial for maintaining the trust of shareholders, investors, and other stakeholders. Transparency also helps in detecting any fraudulent or unethical activities and taking appropriate measures to prevent them.

Why financial stability is crucial for long-term success

Financial stability is essential for long-term success for several reasons. It provides individuals with the ability to plan and achieve their long-term goals, ensures a sense of security and stability, and allows for more opportunities and options. In this essay, we will discuss in detail why financial stability is crucial for long-term success.

First and foremost, financial stability allows individuals to plan and achieve their long-term goals. When one has their finances in order, they have a clear understanding of their income, expenses, and savings. This enables them to set realistic and achievable goals for the future, such as purchasing a home, starting a business, or saving for retirement. Without financial stability, it is challenging to make long-term plans and achieve them successfully. Unstable finances can lead to constant stress and uncertainty, making it difficult to focus on long-term goals.

Moreover, financial stability ensures a sense of security and stability for individuals and their families. It provides a safety net in case of unforeseen circumstances, such as loss of employment, medical emergencies, or natural disasters. When someone has enough savings and a stable income, they can handle unexpected expenses without risking their long-term financial stability. This security also extends to one's loved ones, as they can be assured that in case of any adversity, their family will be taken care of.

Financial stability also opens up more opportunities and options for individuals. With stable finances, one can afford to invest in their education or pursue their passions and interests without the fear of financial constraints. It also allows for more extensive and better job opportunities, as employers value candidates with a stable financial background. Furthermore, individuals with financial stability can afford to take calculated risks, such as starting a business, which can lead to long-term success and financial growth.

Moreover, financial stability helps individuals to maintain a good credit score, which is crucial for long-term success. A good credit score opens up opportunities for loans, mortgages, and credit cards, which can be used to invest in assets that appreciate in value, such as a home or stocks. A good credit score also reflects responsible financial management, which can open up more doors for career and personal growth opportunities.

Lastly, financial stability leads to peace of mind and overall well-being. It eliminates the stress and anxiety that come with financial instability, which can negatively impact one's physical and mental health. With financial stability, individuals can focus on personal and career growth, as maintaining a healthy work-life balance, without worrying about their finances.

Principles for managing finances effectively

Managing finances effectively is essential for both individuals and organizations to achieve financial stability and success. Effective financial management requires a thorough understanding of financial principles and the ability to create and follow a sound financial plan.

Below are the key principles for managing finances effectively:

Set Clear Financial Goals:

The first step towards effective financial management is setting clear and achievable financial goals. These goals should be specific, measurable, and time-bound. For individuals, financial goals can include saving for retirement, paying off debt, and building an emergency fund. For organizations, financial goals can include increasing profits, reducing costs, and improving cash flow.

Create a Budget:
A budget is a plan that outlines income and expenses over a specific period. It helps individuals and organizations track their spending and stay within their means. A budget should be realistic and based on the financial goals set. It should also be regularly reviewed and adjusted as needed.

Track and Monitor Spending:
Tracking spending is crucial for managing finances effectively. It helps identify areas where money is being spent unnecessarily and allows for adjustments to be made to stay within the budget. This can be done by regularly reviewing bank statements and

expenses, keeping receipts, and using budgeting tools or apps.

Save and Invest Wisely:
Saving and investing are key components of effective financial management. It is important to have savings for unexpected expenses and emergencies. Additionally, investing can help grow savings and generate passive income. The key is to be informed and make wise investment decisions based on risk tolerance and financial goals.

Manage Debt:
Debt can be a major obstacle in achieving financial stability. Therefore, managing debt effectively is crucial for managing finances effectively. This includes creating a plan to pay off debt, prioritizing high-interest debt, and avoiding taking on unnecessary debt.

Diversify Income:
Relying on a single source of income can be risky. It is essential to have multiple sources of income to secure financial stability. This can include a side hustle, investments, or passive income streams.

Review and Adjust:

Financial management is an ongoing process. It is important to review and adjust financial plans regularly to ensure they align with changing goals and circumstances. For organizations, this can include conducting financial audits and implementing cost-saving measures. For individuals, this can involve reassessing savings and investment plans.

Seek Professional Advice:

Managing finances effectively can be challenging, and seeking professional advice can be beneficial. Financial advisors, accountants, and lawyers can provide valuable insights and guidance in creating and managing financial plans.

Investing for the future

Investing for the future is one of the smartest and most responsible decisions one can make in today's world. It involves setting aside a portion of one's income and putting it towards long-term financial goals such as retirement, education, buying a house, or creating a source of passive income. By doing so, one can secure their financial future and ensure a comfortable and stress-free life.

The concept of investing for the future is based on the idea of saving and growing money over an extended period of time. It is a crucial aspect of personal finance and requires discipline, patience, and a well-thought-out strategy. It is not just limited to buying stocks or real estate but encompasses a broader range of assets such as mutual funds, bonds, certificates of deposits, and even cryptocurrencies.

One of the primary reasons for investing for the future is to achieve financial security. In today's world, relying solely on a regular job or a fixed income is not enough to sustain oneself, especially in the long run. Inflation, rising cost of living, and unforeseen emergencies can significantly impact one's financial stability. By investing, one can create a financial safety net and ensure that they are prepared for any contingencies.

Another crucial aspect of investing for the future is creating wealth. Instead of just earning to meet one's current needs, investing allows one to generate more money over time. With the right investment choices, one can earn a return on their initial investment, and these earnings can be reinvested to create a compounded effect, significantly increasing one's wealth in the long run.

Investing for the future also allows for the fulfillment of long-term goals. Many people dream of buying a house, sending their children to a good college, or retiring early. These goals require a substantial amount of money, and investing is one of the best ways to achieve them. By starting early and consistently investing, one can reap the benefits of compounding and achieve their goals within a specific timeframe.

Moreover, investing for the future also provides a sense of financial freedom and independence. It allows one to break away from the cycle of living paycheck to paycheck and opens up opportunities for new experiences such as traveling, pursuing a passion, or starting a business. It also provides a sense of security for one's loved ones, as the wealth created through investing can be passed down to future generations.

However, investing for the future is not without risks. There is always a certain level of risk associated with any investment, and it is crucial to understand and manage these risks before making any investment decisions. This is where the role of financial advisors and experts comes in. Seeking professional advice can help in developing a well-diversified investment portfolio that suits one's financial goals, risk appetite, and time horizon.

Conclusively, investing for the future is a vital aspect of personal finance that should not be overlooked. It provides a means to secure one's financial future, create wealth, and achieve long-term goals. With proper planning, discipline, and the right investment choices, one can pave the way for a comfortable and fulfilling life. Therefore, it is essential to start investing early and consistently to reap the maximum benefits in the future.

Understanding the importance of investing

Investing is often seen as a daunting and risky task by many individuals, and therefore, it is largely overlooked or put off until later in life. However, understanding the importance of investing is crucial for achieving financial stability and reaching long-term financial goals. By investing, one can build wealth, create a passive income stream, and secure a comfortable retirement.

Building long-term wealth is perhaps the most well-known benefit of investing. It allows one to grow their money over time through various investment vehicles such as stocks, bonds, real estate, and mutual funds. Unlike traditional savings methods, which offer low-interest rates, investing has the potential to generate significantly higher returns. By starting early and taking calculated risks, the power of compounding can significantly increase one's investment returns over time.

Investing is also an effective way to create a passive income stream. Passive income refers to income earned without actively working for it. It is generated from the interest, dividends, and capital gains earned from investments. By building a diverse investment portfolio, one can earn a steady stream of income, enabling them to achieve financial independence and pursue other interests beyond their regular job.

Moreover, investing is an essential aspect of retirement planning. With the rise in life expectancy, people are now spending a longer part of their life in retirement. To maintain the same standard of living in retirement, it is crucial to start investing early on. It allows one to save and accumulate funds over a longer period, providing financial security during retirement.

Apart from financial benefits, investing also helps in protecting one's assets and savings from inflation. With inflation, the prices of goods and services rise, and the value of money decreases. By investing in assets that adjust to inflation, such as stocks, real estate, and commodities, one can protect their wealth and potentially even increase it.

While investing carries some level of risk, it is important to understand that the risk can be managed through proper research and diversification of investments. By investing in a mix of low-risk and high-risk assets, one can minimize the overall risk and achieve a balance between growth and security.

Overall, understanding the importance of investing allows individuals to take control of their financial future. It helps in building wealth, creating a passive income stream, securing a retirement plan, and protecting against inflation. By starting early, taking calculated risks, and diversifying one's investments, individuals can reap the benefits of investing and achieve their long-term financial goals.

Strategies for making wise investments

Investing is an essential part of financial planning and can help individuals achieve their long-term financial goals. However, with the vast array of investment options available, it can be challenging to determine which strategies will lead to wise investments. While there is no one right formula for making wise investments, there are some key strategies that can help individuals make sound decisions and achieve their investment objectives. In this article, we will discuss some essential strategies for making wise investments.

Define your investment objectives and risk tolerance

Before investing, it is crucial to define your investment objectives and risk tolerance. Investment objectives can vary from short-term goals such as buying a house or going on a holiday to long-term goals like planning for retirement or your child's education. Your investment objectives will impact the type of investment you choose and your investment time horizon.

Risk tolerance refers to your willingness and ability to bear losses in your investment portfolio. Some individuals have a high-risk tolerance and are comfortable investing in high-risk, high-reward investments, while others prefer lower-risk, steady investments. Understanding your risk tolerance is crucial to choosing the right investment strategy.

Diversify your investments

One of the most critical strategies for making wise investments is diversification. Diversifying your investments means spreading your money across different types of assets, such as stocks, bonds, real estate, and commodities. Diversification can help mitigate risk, as losses in one asset can be offset by gains in another. It is essential to diversify not only across different assets but also within each asset class. For example, diversifying your stock portfolio across different industries and companies can help reduce the risk of losing your investment if one company or industry performs poorly.

Have a long-term perspective

Investing is a long-term game, and successful investors understand the importance of having a long-term perspective. It is essential to resist the temptation to make hasty and emotional decisions based on short-term market fluctuations. Instead, focus on your long-term goals and make informed decisions based on your investment objectives and risk tolerance.

Conduct thorough research and due diligence

Before making any investment, it is imperative to conduct thorough research and due diligence on the investment opportunity. This includes researching the company or asset you are investing in, its financial performance, management team, and potential risks. If you are investing in mutual funds or other managed investment products, research the fund manager's track record and investment strategy.

Keep emotions in check

Emotions can be a significant barrier to making wise investments. Greed, fear, and overconfidence can cause investors to make impulsive and irrational decisions. It is crucial to keep emotions in check and make logical and rational decisions based on facts and research.

Consider dollar-cost averaging

Dollar-cost averaging is a strategy that involves investing a fixed amount of money at regular intervals, such as monthly or quarterly, regardless of the market's ups and downs. This strategy can help investors reduce the risk of buying at the market's peak and help them benefit from market dips.

Seek professional advice

Investing can be a complex and overwhelming process, especially for beginners. Seeking professional advice from a financial advisor can help individuals make wise investment decisions based on their goals and risk profile. A financial advisor can also provide valuable insights and guidance on selecting investments, diversifying your portfolio, and managing your investments.

In general, making wise investments requires a combination of understanding your investment objectives, diversifying your portfolio, staying disciplined, conducting thorough research, and seeking professional advice. By incorporating these strategies into your investment plan, you can increase your chances of making wise investments and achieving your long-term financial goals. Remember that investing is a journey, and it is essential to stay informed and reassess your investment strategy regularly to ensure it aligns with your goals and risk tolerance.

Budgeting and saving money

Budgeting is a crucial aspect of managing personal finances that enables individuals to make informed decisions when it comes to spending and saving money. It involves creating a detailed plan for how one's income will be divided and allocated towards various expenses and savings goals. Effective budgeting helps individuals to live within their means, achieve financial stability, and work towards long-term financial goals.

The first step in budgeting is to track one's income and expenses. This involves keeping a record of all the sources of income, including salaries, bonuses, and any other forms of income. On the other hand, expenses should be categorized into fixed and variable expenses. Fixed expenses are those that remain the same every month, such as rent, mortgage, and insurance premiums, while variable expenses are those that fluctuate, such as groceries, entertainment, and clothing. Tracking expenses for a few months helps to identify unnecessary spending and prioritize essential expenses.

Once income and expenses have been tracked, the next step is to create a budget. The budget should include all sources of income and allocate the funds towards various expenses and savings goals. It is essential to be realistic when creating a budget and ensure that expenses do not exceed income. If there is a surplus, it can be allocated towards savings or paying off debts.

Setting financial goals is an integral part of effective budgeting. Having specific and measurable goals motivates individuals to stick to their budget and remain focused on their long-term financial objectives. These goals can be short-term, such as paying off credit card debt within a year, or long-term, such as saving for a down payment on a house or retirement.

Budgeting also requires making necessary adjustments from time to time. It is normal for unexpected expenses to arise, and a budget should be flexible enough to accommodate these changes. For example, if a medical emergency arises, funds can be reallocated from other categories to cover the expenses.

One of the main benefits of budgeting is that it enables individuals to save money. By having a clear understanding of where the money is going, individuals can identify areas where they can cut back on expenses and increase their savings. This could involve finding cheaper alternatives for everyday expenses, such as groceries or utilities, or cutting back on discretionary spending.

Another important aspect of budgeting is creating an emergency fund. This is a separate savings account that can cover unexpected expenses such as car repairs, medical emergencies, or job loss. Ideally, one should have enough funds to cover three to six months' worth of expenses in their emergency fund.

Budgeting also helps individuals to avoid debt or work towards paying off existing debt. By prioritizing essential expenses and saving money, individuals can reduce their reliance on credit cards or loans. This, in turn, prevents them from falling into a cycle of debt and accruing interest charges.

In addition to saving money, budgeting can also help individuals to invest in their future. Whether it is building a retirement fund, investing in stocks or property, having a budget allows individuals to allocate funds towards long-term investments and build wealth over time.

There are several tools available to help individuals with budgeting. These include budgeting apps, spreadsheets, or even a simple pen and paper. The key is to find a method that works best for an individual and to stick to it consistently.

Budgeting is a critical aspect of managing personal finances that allows individuals to live within their means, save money, and work towards long-term financial goals. It requires tracking income and expenses, setting financial goals, and making necessary adjustments. By budgeting effectively, individuals can gain control of their finances and achieve financial stability.

Styles for creating and sticking to a budget

A budget is an essential tool for managing personal finances. It helps individuals to track their income, expenses, and savings, enabling them to make informed financial decisions and achieve their financial goals. Creating and sticking to a budget requires a certain style or approach, as not everyone has the same spending habits and financial priorities. In this essay, we will discuss some of the styles for creating and sticking to a budget.

The Traditional Style

This is the most common budgeting style, where individuals use a pen and paper or a spreadsheet to record their income and expenses. The traditional style involves creating a monthly budget by listing down all the sources of income and fixed expenses such as rent, utilities, and insurance. Then, individuals estimate their variable expenses such as groceries, dining out, and entertainment. This style requires individuals to review their budget regularly and adjust their spending accordingly. It is a simple yet effective way of budgeting that can work for people who prefer a more hands-on approach.

The Envelope System

The envelope system is a cash-based budgeting style that involves dividing cash into different envelopes, each representing a specific expense category such as groceries, entertainment, and transportation. This style works well for those who struggle with overspending and impulse purchases. Once the cash in an envelope is exhausted, individuals cannot spend any more in that particular category until the next month. This system creates a visible limit and can help individuals control their spending and stick to a budget.

The Zero-Based Budget

The zero-based budgeting style is based on the principle of allocating every penny of income towards a specific expense or savings goal. In this style, individuals allocate their income towards needs, wants, and savings. The goal is to ensure that every dollar is accounted for, and there is no money left at the end of the month. This style requires individuals to plan their spending carefully and prioritize their expenses. It can be a useful tool for those who want to be more intentional with their spending and savings.

The 50/30/20 Budget

The 50/30/20 budget is a popular budgeting method that involves allocating 50% of income towards needs, 30% towards wants, and 20% towards savings and debt repayment. The idea behind this style is to find a balance between necessary expenses and discretionary spending while still saving for the future. It is a simple and flexible budgeting style that can work well for those who have a hard time sticking to a strict budget.

The Mobile App Style

In today's digital age, there are several budgeting apps available that can help individuals track their expenses and savings easily. These apps allow users to link their bank accounts and credit cards to automatically track their spending. They also provide budgeting tips and personalized insights to help users stick to their budget. This style is suitable for those who are tech-savvy and prefer a more hands-off approach to budgeting.

In conclusion, there is no one-size-fits-all approach to creating and sticking to a budget. Different styles work for different individuals based on their spending habits, financial priorities, and personal preferences. The key is to find a budgeting style that works for you and stick to it consistently. Budgeting takes discipline and commitment, but the rewards of financial stability and achieving your goals far outweigh the effort put into it.

Part ways to save money for future goals and investments

Saving money is a crucial aspect of achieving financial stability and securing future goals and investments. It not only helps to cover any unexpected expenses but also allows individuals to plan for their long-term financial goals. Saving money involves discipline, sacrifices, and a proper understanding of financial planning. With diligent effort, one can achieve financial stability and achieve their future financial goals with ease.

Here are some effective ways to save money for future goals and investments:

Set clear and achievable goals: The first step towards saving money is to set clear and achievable financial goals. This will help in determining the amount of money needed to be saved and the time frame to achieve the goals. It could include buying a house, saving for retirement, starting a business, or any other long-term investment.

Create a budget: A budget is a crucial tool for managing expenses and saving money. It helps in tracking the income and expenses, thereby giving a clear picture of where the money is being spent. By creating a budget, individuals can identify unnecessary expenses and make necessary adjustments to save more money.

Prioritize saving: It is essential to make saving a priority. As soon as the income is received, a certain portion of it should be saved before any expenses are made. This ensures that saving becomes a habit and individuals can reach their financial goals faster.

Reduce unnecessary expenses: Cutting down on unnecessary expenses can significantly increase savings. It could be as simple as opting for homemade meals instead of eating out, cancelling unused subscriptions, or finding ways to reduce utility bills. This will not only save money but also help to adopt a more sustainable and frugal lifestyle.

Automate savings: Automation of savings is an effective way to save money regularly. With this, a specified amount of money is automatically transferred to a savings account every month. This eliminates the need for manual transfers and ensures that saving is done consistently.

Invest wisely: Investing is an excellent way to grow savings and achieve long-term financial goals. It is essential to research and understand the investment options available, such as stocks, mutual funds, real estate, etc. One can seek the help of a financial advisor to make informed investment decisions.

Avoid debt: Debt, especially high-interest debt, can hinder savings and delay future goals and investments. It is crucial to avoid getting into debt by living within one's means and avoiding unnecessary loans and credit card expenses.

Be disciplined: Saving money requires discipline and consistency. It is essential to stick to the budget and avoid impulsive purchases. It is also crucial to regularly track the progress of savings and make necessary adjustments to reach financial goals on time.

Take advantage of tax benefits: There are various tax benefits available for long-term savings and investments. It is advisable to research and understand these benefits to maximize savings and minimize taxes.

Always have an emergency fund: It is essential to have an emergency fund to cover unexpected expenses and financial emergencies. This fund should ideally cover at least 3-6 months of expenses and should be separate from the savings for future goals and investments.

Generally, saving money for future goals and investments requires discipline, a well-planned budget, and wise investment decisions. By following these tips and making saving a priority, individuals can achieve financial stability and reach their financial goals with ease. It is important to remember that saving money takes time and effort, but the long-term benefits and financial security it provides are worth it.

Chapter 10
Leadership Skills

Leadership skills refer to a set of qualities and behaviors that enable an individual to effectively guide and influence others towards a common goal or vision. These skills include the ability to communicate effectively, make sound decisions, inspire and motivate team members, and adapt to changing circumstances.

One important aspect of leadership skills is communication. This involves not only being able to clearly articulate ideas and expectations, but also actively listening to others and providing feedback. Effective communication allows leaders to build strong relationships with their team and foster a sense of trust and collaboration.

Another critical element of leadership skills is decision making. Leaders must be able to make well-informed and timely decisions, considering the opinions and needs of their team and stakeholders. They should also be able to handle pressure and uncertainty, and take responsibility for the outcomes of their decisions.

Leadership also involves the ability to inspire and motivate others towards a common goal. This requires a positive attitude, strong work ethic, and the ability to lead by example. A good leader should also be able to recognize and utilize the strengths of each team member, encouraging them to reach their full potential.

Finally, strong leadership skills include the ability to adapt to changing circumstances and overcome challenges. This involves being flexible, open to new ideas, and able to think creatively to find solutions. In times of crisis or uncertainty, effective leaders remain calm and focused, providing a sense of stability and direction for their team.

Overall, leadership skills are essential for anyone in a position of authority or influence. They allow individuals to effectively guide and support their team, create a positive work culture, and achieve common goals. These skills can be learned and developed over time, making it possible for anyone to become an effective leader.

Characteristics of effective leaders

Effective leadership is a crucial aspect of any successful organization. It involves leading a team towards a common goal, making important decisions, and influencing others to achieve desired outcomes. While different leadership styles and approaches exist, there are certain characteristics that are commonly found in effective leaders. In this essay, we will discuss the characteristics of effective leaders and their importance in achieving success.

Visionary: An effective leader has a clear and compelling vision for the future. They are able to articulate this vision to their team and inspire them to work towards it. A leader with a strong vision is able to see the big picture and can make decisions that align with the long-term goals of the organization.

Integrity and authenticity: Effective leaders are known for their integrity and authenticity. They lead by example and are transparent in their actions and decisions. This builds trust and credibility among their team members, which is essential for effective leadership.

Effective communication: Communication is a crucial aspect of leadership. Effective leaders are skilled communicators who are able to convey their ideas, expectations, and feedback clearly and effectively. They also actively listen to their team members and make an effort to understand their perspectives.

Empathy and emotional intelligence: Empathy is the ability to understand and share the feelings of others. Effective leaders possess high levels of emotional intelligence, which allows them to empathize with their team, understand their emotions, and respond appropriately. This helps to create a positive and supportive work environment.

Decisiveness: Effective leaders are decisive and able to make tough decisions when needed. They gather all the relevant information, weigh the pros and cons, and make timely and well-informed decisions. This helps to keep the team on track and ensures that goals are achieved in a timely manner.

Adaptability: The ability to adapt to changing circumstances is another important characteristic of effective leaders. They are flexible and open-minded, willing to embrace new ideas and approaches to achieve success. This also allows them to respond to unexpected challenges and setbacks effectively.

Accountability: Effective leaders take responsibility for their actions and decisions. They hold themselves accountable for the outcomes of their team and are willing to learn from their mistakes. This creates a culture of accountability within the team, leading to increased productivity and a focus on continuous improvement.

Empowers and delegates: Effective leaders understand that they cannot achieve success alone and therefore, they delegate tasks to their team members based on their strengths and abilities. They also empower their team members by providing them with the necessary resources, support, and autonomy to do their jobs effectively.

Lifelong learners: Truly effective leaders are lifelong learners and are constantly seeking ways to improve their skills and knowledge. They invest in their personal and professional development and encourage their team members to do the same. This mindset of continuous learning and improvement helps to keep the team and organization ahead of the competition.

Resilience and positivity: Lastly, effective leaders possess a positive attitude and are able to maintain their composure in the face of challenges and setbacks. They are resilient and are able to bounce back from failures and setbacks, inspiring their team to do the same.

Effective leadership is a combination of various characteristics such as vision, integrity, effective communication, empathy, adaptability, and accountability. These qualities allow leaders to motivate, inspire, and guide their team towards achieving success. It is important for aspiring leaders to develop and nurture these characteristics to become effective leaders.

Key traits of successful leaders

Successful leaders possess a unique set of qualities and characteristics that set them apart from others. These key traits enable them to inspire, motivate, and lead their team towards achieving a common goal. In this essay, we will discuss the top key traits of successful leaders.

Vision and Strategic Thinking

A successful leader is someone who has a clear vision and is able to think strategically. They have a long-term perspective and are able to see the bigger picture. They have a well-defined plan and are always looking ahead to identify potential challenges and opportunities. This enables them to make decisions that align with their vision and effectively guide their team towards achieving their goals.

Strong Communication Skills

Another key trait of successful leaders is effective communication skills. They are able to articulate their vision, ideas, and expectations clearly and concisely. They are also good listeners, creating an environment of open communication and fostering a sense of trust and respect among their team. Moreover, successful leaders are adaptable communicators, able to adjust their style of communication to suit different situations and audiences.

Empathy and Emotional Intelligence

Successful leaders have a high level of emotional intelligence and possess empathy towards their team. They understand the importance of building strong relationships and foster a culture of empathy and collaboration in their organization. They are able to connect with their team on a personal level, which helps in creating a positive and productive work environment.

Decisiveness

Being decisive and having the ability to make tough decisions is a crucial trait of a successful leader. They are not afraid to take risks and make difficult choices for the betterment of their team and organization. Successful leaders have a strong sense of judgment and are able to weigh the pros and cons before making a decision. They also take responsibility for their decisions and are able to learn from their mistakes.

Passion and Resilience

Passion is a key trait of all successful leaders. They are driven by their love for what they do, and this passion motivates their team to achieve greatness. Additionally, successful leaders are resilient and are able to persevere through challenges and setbacks. They see failures as opportunities to learn and grow and do not let them discourage or demotivate themselves or their team.

Accountability and Integrity

Successful leaders understand the importance of accountability and lead by example. They take ownership of their actions and decisions, and they expect the same from their team. They also uphold a high standard of integrity, following ethical and moral principles in their leadership. This builds trust and credibility among their team and stakeholders.

Continuous Learning

Another key trait of a successful leader is their thirst for knowledge and continuous learning. They understand that the world is constantly evolving, and to stay ahead, they must be open to new ideas and ways of thinking. They are lifelong learners and encourage their team to do the same. This helps in keeping their organization relevant and innovative.

Successful leaders possess a combination of these key traits that enable them to effectively lead their team towards success. They are visionaries, effective communicators, empathetic, decisive, passionate, resilient, accountable, and lifelong learners. These traits are not something one is born with, but they can be developed and honed through dedication and hard work.

How to develop and strengthen leadership skills

Leadership is an essential skill that is necessary for success in any field or aspect of life. Whether in a professional setting, personal relationships, or social and community engagements, strong leadership skills are vital for effective decision-making, problem-solving, and overall growth and development. However, leadership skills do not come naturally to everyone, and just like any other skill, they require development and continuous improvement. In this article, we will discuss how one can develop and strengthen their leadership skills.

Understand Your Personal Leadership Style

The first step in developing leadership skills is understanding your personal leadership style. There are various theories and models of leadership, such as servant leadership, transformational leadership, and situational leadership. These styles have different approaches to leading and motivating teams. It is essential to assess your strengths, weaknesses, and values to determine which style aligns with your personality and goals. This self-awareness will help you develop a leadership style that is authentic and effective.

Seek out Leadership Training and Development Opportunities

There are numerous opportunities for leadership training and development, both online and offline. Look for workshops, seminars, courses, or conferences that focus on leadership skills. These programs will not only expose you to various perspectives and theories of leadership, but they also provide practical tools and strategies for effective leadership. Additionally, these programs offer networking opportunities with other aspiring leaders and established professionals who can serve as mentors and provide valuable insights and guidance.

Reflect on Past Leadership Experiences

Another effective way to develop and strengthen leadership skills is by reflecting on past leadership experiences. Think about times when you took charge or led a team. What was the outcome? What did you do well, and what could you have done differently? Reflecting on these experiences helps you identify your strengths and weaknesses as a leader and provides a basis for improvement and growth. Also, seek feedback from team members, colleagues, or mentors on your leadership style and areas for improvement.

Read and Learn from Successful Leaders

Reading about the experiences and practices of successful leaders can be a valuable learning tool. There are numerous books, articles, and blogs written by accomplished leaders that can provide insights and guidance on effective leadership. By studying their strategies, techniques, and philosophies, you can adapt and incorporate them into your own leadership style. Additionally, joining a leadership book club or discussion group can provide a forum for dialogue and exchange of ideas on leadership principles.

Embrace Continuous Learning and Improvement

Leadership skills, like any other skill, require continuous learning and improvement. The business and social landscapes are constantly evolving, and as a leader, you must keep up with the latest trends, technologies, and strategies to remain effective. Attend webinars, workshops, and conferences, read articles, listen to podcasts, and engage in discussions on leadership topics to stay informed and continuously improve your skills.

Practice Active Listening

Effective communication is a critical aspect of leadership. It is essential to be an active listener to understand the needs, concerns, and perspectives of team members. This involves listening attentively, asking clarifying questions, and paraphrasing what you have heard to ensure you understand correctly. Active listening fosters trust and respect among team members and helps you make informed decisions and provide effective guidance.

Take on Leadership Roles and Responsibilities

Experience is a significant factor in developing and strengthening leadership skills. Take on leadership roles in your workplace, community, or social groups to gain practical experience in leading and managing people. This could involve leading a project, chairing a committee, or mentoring a colleague. These experiences will help you apply the knowledge you have acquired and gain valuable insights into your leadership abilities.

Lead by Example

A fundamental aspect of leadership is leading by example. As a leader, your actions, values, and ethos should align with the goals and values of your team or organization. This consistency builds trust and respect among team members, and they are more likely to follow your lead and work towards common objectives. Additionally, by setting a good example, you inspire others to develop their leadership skills and become leaders themselves.

In general, developing and strengthening leadership skills is an ongoing process that requires dedication, self-awareness, and continuous learning. By understanding your personal leadership style, seeking out learning opportunities, reflecting on past experiences, and practicing effective communication, you can become a successful and influential leader. Additionally, leading by example, embracing continuous learning, and taking on leadership roles will help you grow and improve your skills as a leader. As John C. Maxwell once said, "Leadership is not about titles, positions, or flowcharts. It is about one life influencing another." By developing and strengthening your leadership skills, you can positively influence the lives of those around you and achieve success in all aspects of your life.

Delegating tasks and empowering others

Delegating tasks and empowering others are essential skills for any successful leader or manager. In today's fast-paced and complex working environment, it is impossible for one person to handle all the responsibilities and tasks on their own. Delegating tasks not only helps in reducing the workload but also empowers team members to take ownership and responsibility for their work, ultimately increasing productivity and achieving organizational goals.

Delegating tasks involves assigning specific tasks and responsibilities to team members according to their strengths, skills, and expertise while empowering others is an ongoing process of giving employees the authority, autonomy and support to make decisions and take action.

One of the key benefits of delegating tasks is that it allows leaders to focus on their high-priority tasks and strategic initiatives.

By entrusting tasks to others, leaders can avoid getting overwhelmed and can utilize their time and energy on important tasks that cannot be delegated. This not only improves their efficiency but also ensures that all tasks are being handled with equal importance.

In addition, delegating tasks to team members can help in their personal and professional growth. By giving them new tasks and challenges, employees are encouraged to learn new skills and develop their strengths. This not only increases their job satisfaction but also helps in nurturing future leaders within the organization.

Empowering others is also crucial for building a strong and motivated team. When employees are given the authority to make decisions and take action, they feel trusted and valued. This boosts their confidence and motivation, making them more committed to their work and the organization. Moreover, it fosters a sense of ownership and accountability among employees, leading to better results and outcomes.

Delegating tasks and empowering others can also help in creating a positive work culture. When leaders delegate tasks and involve team members in decision-making, it promotes collaboration, open communication, and mutual respect within the team. This not only improves team dynamics but also promotes a sense of belonging and teamwork.

Moreover, delegating tasks helps in building a diverse and inclusive workplace. By assigning tasks to individuals with different backgrounds, experiences, and perspectives, leaders can tap into their unique strengths and ideas, leading to innovative solutions and a variety of approaches to problem-solving.

However, to ensure successful delegation and empowerment, leaders need to communicate effectively. This involves setting clear expectations, providing necessary resources and support, and giving feedback and recognition for a job well done. By doing so, leaders can build trust and transparency with their team members and prevent miscommunications or misunderstandings.

Importance of delegation in effective leadership

Delegation is the process of entrusting a task or responsibility to another individual or group, while still remaining accountable for its completion. In effective leadership, delegation plays a crucial role in achieving organizational goals and maximizing team productivity. It is a skill that sets effective leaders apart from inefficient ones, as it not only benefits the leader but also the team and the organization as a whole. Successful delegation requires trust, effective communication, and a clear understanding of individual strengths and weaknesses. In this essay, we will discuss the importance of delegation in effective leadership.

Firstly, delegation allows leaders to focus on high-level tasks and strategic thinking. Leaders are responsible for overseeing the overall direction and success of their team or organization. With a variety of tasks and responsibilities on their plate, leaders often struggle to find the time and energy to focus on important tasks that require their expertise and decision-making abilities. By delegating tasks to capable team members, leaders can free up their time and energy to focus on tasks that require their specific skill set. This helps leaders to prioritize their workload and delegate tasks that can be done by others, while still ensuring that all important tasks are completed on time.

Secondly, delegation helps to build trust within the team. A leader who delegates tasks demonstrates trust in their team members' abilities, which in turn, fosters a sense of ownership and responsibility in the team. This creates a positive work environment where individuals feel valued and empowered to take on new challenges. As a result, team members feel motivated to work harder and contribute to the overall success of the organization. On the other hand, leaders who do not delegate can come across as micromanagers, which can lead to employee demotivation and a lack of trust in their abilities.

Moreover, delegation enables effective utilization of resources. In any organization, time, money, and human resources are valuable and limited. By delegating tasks to team members who have the necessary skills and knowledge, leaders can ensure that resources are used efficiently. This leads to better time management and cost-effective solutions, as tasks are divided among individuals who are best suited to complete them. Additionally, delegation helps to develop and utilize the full potential of team members. By giving team members new and challenging tasks to work on, leaders can help them develop new skills and expand their knowledge and expertise. This not only benefits the individual but also adds value to the organization by creating a more diverse and skilled workforce.

Furthermore, delegation promotes a culture of collaboration. In delegating tasks, leaders are creating opportunities for team members to work together, share ideas and knowledge, and seek support from each other. This not only improves team coordination but also leads to better decision-making and problem-solving. Team members are more likely to come up with innovative solutions when they are working together and utilizing each other's strengths. This results in higher productivity and a more efficient workflow, ultimately contributing to the organization's success.

Delegation is a vital aspect of effective leadership. It allows leaders to focus on important tasks, builds trust and fosters a positive work environment, optimizes resource utilization, and promotes collaboration within the team. By delegating tasks effectively, leaders can improve their own and their team's performance, leading to the overall success of the organization. Effective delegation is a skill that every leader should possess, and it is an essential component of strong and successful leadership.

Tips for delegating tasks and empowering team members

As a leader, it can be tempting to handle all tasks and decisions on your own. However, this can lead to burnout and limit the growth and development of your team members. Delegating tasks and empowering team members is crucial for a successful and efficient team. Here are some tips to help you effectively delegate tasks and empower your team members:

Understand your team members' skills and strengths: The first step is to have a clear understanding of your team members' skills, abilities, and strengths. This will help you assign tasks that align with their expertise and also ensure that they feel confident while performing the tasks. It will also allow you to identify areas where they need more support or training.

Establish clear expectations: When delegating tasks, it is essential to set clear expectations. This includes clearly defining the task, its purpose, and the desired outcome. You should also establish a timeline and discuss any specific guidelines or standards that need to be followed. This will help your team members understand what is expected of them and work towards achieving the desired results.

Communicate effectively: Proper communication is crucial when delegating tasks. It is important to explain the task clearly and provide all the necessary information. Make sure to answer any questions and address any concerns your team members may have. Effective communication also involves giving regular feedback and updates on the progress of the task.

Encourage creativity and autonomy: When delegating tasks, it is important to trust your team members' abilities and give them the autonomy to make decisions and find creative solutions. This will not only make them feel valued and empowered but also bring fresh ideas and perspectives to the team.

Provide necessary resources: To ensure your team members can complete the delegated tasks successfully, it is essential to provide them with the necessary resources and support. This includes tools, training, and any other resources needed to complete the task effectively. Lack of resources can lead to frustration and demotivation, hindering the success of the task.

Celebrate successes and learn from failures: It is important to celebrate the successful completion of tasks and give credit to the team members responsible. This will boost morale and motivate them to take on more responsibilities in the future. In case of failures, make sure to have a discussion and identify the reasons for the failure. This will help your team members learn from their mistakes and improve their performance in the future.

Be open to feedback: Delegating tasks also involves being open to feedback from your team members. Encourage them to share their thoughts and ideas and listen to their suggestions. This will not only make them feel valued but also bring new insights and perspectives to the team.

Lead by example: As a leader, it is important to set an example for your team members. Instead of just delegating tasks, show them how to do it by leading from the front. This will not only motivate them but also build trust and respect within the team.

Infact, delegating tasks and empowering team members is crucial for a successful and efficient team. As a leader, it is your responsibility to create a collaborative and supportive environment where team members can grow and excel in their roles. By following these tips and effectively delegating tasks, you can foster a culture of trust, respect, and motivation within your team.

Conflict resolution

Conflict resolution refers to the process of addressing and resolving disputes or disagreements between individuals, groups, or organizations in an amicable and mutually beneficial way. Conflicts are inevitable in any human interaction, whether in personal relationships, the workplace, or society. Therefore, the ability to effectively resolve conflicts is a crucial skill that promotes healthy relationships and enables the progression of work and society.

The first step in resolving conflicts is acknowledging that they exist. Oftentimes, people tend to ignore or avoid conflicts, hoping they will resolve themselves, which only leads to the issue escalating further. Instead, it is essential to have an open and honest discussion to identify the root cause of the conflict. Each party involved should have the opportunity to express their perspective and feelings without interruption or judgment. This allows for a better understanding of both sides and creates a sense of empathy and mutual respect.

The next step is to actively listen to each other with an open mind. It is crucial to hear out each party's concerns and opinions without bias or assumptions. Listening attentively can help uncover the underlying reasons for the conflict and reveal potential solutions. Each party should also communicate clearly and respectfully, avoiding aggressive or accusatory language that can further escalate the situation.

Once the issues have been clearly identified and understood, it is time to work towards finding a resolution. This involves brainstorming and considering different ideas and perspectives to find a mutually beneficial solution. It is essential to focus on finding a win-win situation, where both parties can walk away feeling satisfied and respected. Compromises may need to be made, and it is crucial to be flexible and open to alternative solutions.

It is also necessary to keep emotions in check during conflict resolution. Emotions can often cloud judgment and lead to impulsive decisions or hurtful words. Both parties should strive to remain calm and composed, even during the most heated discussions. Taking breaks and practicing relaxation techniques, like deep breathing and mindfulness, can help manage emotions and avoid saying or doing something regrettable.

Finally, it is essential to follow through with the agreed-upon solution. This means actively implementing the resolution and monitoring its effectiveness. It is also crucial to communicate and reaffirm the commitment to maintaining the resolution to prevent the same issues from recurring in the future.

Strategies for resolving conflicts and promoting a positive work environment

Conflicts are an inevitable part of any workplace, but if not handled properly, they can have a negative impact on employee morale and overall productivity. Therefore, it is crucial for organizations to have effective strategies in place to resolve conflicts and promote a positive work environment. In this essay, we will discuss some of the strategies that can be adopted to manage conflicts and create a harmonious and collaborative workplace.

Encourage open communication: Effective communication is the key to resolving conflicts. Encourage open and transparent communication among employees, this will help in addressing the issues at an early stage before they escalate into a major conflict. Employees should feel comfortable expressing their views and concerns without any fear of repercussions.

Identify the root cause: To effectively resolve a conflict, it is important to identify the root cause of the problem. This will enable the organization to find a suitable solution and prevent similar conflicts from arising in the future. Encourage employees to speak openly about their concerns and actively listen to their points of view to identify the underlying issue.

Promote empathy and understanding: Conflicts often arise due to miscommunication and misunderstandings. Encourage employees to practice empathy and understand each other's perspectives. This will help in creating a supportive and positive work environment where employees respect and value each other's opinions.

Foster a culture of collaboration: Collaboration promotes a sense of teamwork and fosters a culture of trust and respect. Encourage employees to work together towards a common goal, this will help in developing a sense of camaraderie and mitigate conflicts. Also, ensure that credit is given where it is due to avoid feelings of resentment and conflicts among team members.

Train managers and employees in conflict resolution: Conflict resolution is a skill that needs to be developed. Organizations should invest in training their managers and employees in effective conflict resolution techniques. This will not only help in resolving conflicts but also promote a positive work culture where individuals are equipped with the necessary skills to address conflicts in a professional and constructive manner.

Set clear expectations and boundaries: Often conflicts arise due to unclear expectations and boundaries. Make sure that roles, responsibilities, and expectations are clearly defined to avoid any misunderstanding. This will also help in holding individuals accountable for their actions and prevent conflicts from arising.

Encourage a healthy work-life balance: Stress and fatigue can lead to conflicts in the workplace. Encourage employees to maintain a healthy work-life balance by offering flexible work schedules, wellness programs, and time-off. This will not only improve employee morale but also decrease the chances of conflicts.

Lead by example: Leaders play a vital role in setting the tone for the workplace. They should lead by example by practicing effective conflict resolution techniques and promoting a positive work culture. This will help in creating a harmonious and collaborative work environment.

Establish a conflict resolution process: It is important to have a structured process in place to address conflicts. This will help in managing conflicts in a timely and efficient manner. The process should include identifying the issue, understanding each other's perspectives, finding a mutually agreeable solution, and following up to ensure the issue has been resolved.

Encourage feedback and continuous improvement: Finally, it is crucial to encourage open and honest feedback from employees and continuously work towards improving the work environment. This will help in addressing any concerns or conflicts before they become major issues.

In conclusion, conflicts are a natural occurrence in any workplace, but if managed effectively, they can lead to positive outcomes and foster a healthy work environment. By implementing the above-mentioned strategies, organizations can resolve conflicts and promote a culture of collaboration, trust, and respect. This will not only lead to improved employee satisfaction but will also contribute to the overall success of the organization.

Communication techniques for handling difficult situations

Communication can make or break a situation, especially when it comes to handling difficult situations. Whether it's a disagreement with a coworker, a misunderstanding with a friend, or a crisis at work, effective communication techniques can help diffuse tension and find resolutions.

Here are some key communication techniques for handling difficult situations:

Active Listening:
Active listening is crucial in any communication, but especially in difficult situations. It involves really paying attention to what the other person is saying, without interrupting or jumping to conclusions. It also involves reflecting back on what has been said to make sure you understand the other person's perspective. This can help de-escalate a situation and show that you are truly trying to understand and address the issue at hand.

Stay calm and composed:
It's easier said than done, but maintaining a calm and composed demeanor can help de-escalate a difficult situation. When emotions are running high, it's easy to get caught up in the heat of the moment and say or do something that you may regret

later. Taking deep breaths, staying focused and avoiding raising your voice can help keep the situation from getting out of control.

Use "I" statements:
One common mistake people make in difficult situations is using "you" statements, which can come across as accusatory and aggressive. Instead, try using "I" statements, where you express your feelings and perspective without blaming the other person. For example, "I feel upset when you don't listen to my ideas" instead of "You never listen to me!"

Empathize:
Difficult situations often arise due to a difference in perspectives or opinions. Try to put yourself in the other person's shoes and understand their point of view. This can help you approach the situation with empathy and find common ground to work towards a solution.

Focus on the problem, not the person:
When tensions are high, it's easy to make personal attacks and criticize the other

person. However, this only makes the situation worse and can damage the relationship. Instead, focus on the problem at hand and work towards finding a solution together. This helps keep the conversation productive and respectful.

Take a break:
If the situation becomes too overwhelming, it's okay to take a break and come back to it later. Sometimes, a little bit of space and time can help defuse tension and allow both parties to approach the situation with a calmer mindset.

Offer a compromise:
In many difficult situations, there's no one right way to resolve the issue. Instead of insisting on your way, try to come up with a compromise or alternative solution that works for both parties. This shows a willingness to find a mutually agreeable resolution and can help resolve the situation peacefully.

Use nonverbal communication:
Remember that communication is not just about words, but also nonverbal cues such

as body language and tone of voice. To create a positive and open atmosphere, maintain eye contact, use a calm and respectful tone, and avoid crossing your arms or displaying defensive body language.

Follow up:
After the difficult situation has been resolved, it's important to follow up with the other person. This can help reaffirm that the issue has been resolved, and also reinforces the importance of effective communication in maintaining healthy relationships.

Handling difficult situations requires effective communication techniques such as active listening, remaining calm and composed, using "I" statements, and showing empathy. These techniques can help de-escalate tense situations and find mutually agreeable solutions, leading to better relationships and a more positive work or personal environment.

Chapter 11
Continuous self-improvement

Continuous self-improvement, also known as self-development or personal growth, is the practice of constantly striving to improve oneself in various aspects of life. It involves setting goals, identifying strengths and weaknesses, and actively working towards becoming the best version of oneself.

This process of self-improvement is continuous because there is always room for growth and improvement in every area of our lives. It is not a one-time event, but an ongoing journey that requires dedication and effort.

Continuous self-improvement encompasses various areas of life, such as personal, professional, emotional, and spiritual growth. It involves developing new skills, acquiring knowledge, and adopting positive habits that support personal growth.

One of the key benefits of continuous self-improvement is that it leads to a greater sense of self-awareness. By actively seeking ways to improve ourselves, we become more in tune with our strengths, weaknesses, and areas that need growth. This self-awareness allows us to make better decisions, set more meaningful goals, and create a more fulfilling life.

In addition, continuous self-improvement can also lead to increased self-confidence and self-esteem. As we achieve our goals and make progress in our personal growth, we gain a sense of accomplishment and belief in our own abilities.

To engage in continuous self-improvement, it is important to have a growth mindset – a belief that our abilities and talents can be developed through effort and persistence. This mindset allows us to view challenges and setbacks as opportunities for growth, rather than failures.

Some practical ways to practice continuous self-improvement include setting specific and achievable goals, regularly reflecting on our progress and areas for improvement, seeking feedback from others, and investing in personal development activities such as attending workshops or reading self-improvement books.

Importance of continuous self-improvement

Continuous self-improvement, also known as personal growth or self-development, is the process of continuously working on oneself to become a better and more fulfilled individual. It involves actively seeking ways to improve one's skills, knowledge, and personal qualities, and incorporating them into one's daily life. This process is essential for personal as well as professional growth, as it helps individuals to attain their full potential, maximize their strengths, and overcome their weaknesses.

The importance of continuous self-improvement cannot be overstated. In today's fast-paced and constantly evolving world, it is crucial to keep improving oneself to stay competitive and relevant. Here are some reasons why continuous self-improvement is crucial for personal and professional success:

Develops self-awareness: Engaging in continuous self-improvement requires individuals to reflect on their strengths and weaknesses, identify areas that need improvement, and set goals for self-improvement. This process promotes self-awareness, which is essential for understanding one's values, beliefs, and motivations. Self-awareness also allows individuals to identify patterns of behavior and make necessary changes to improve their lives.

Enhances skills and knowledge: Continuous self-improvement involves learning new skills and acquiring knowledge in areas that are relevant to one's personal and professional life. This could include attending workshops, seminars, and training programs, reading books, or taking online courses. By continuously expanding one's skills and knowledge, individuals can increase their value in the job market, advance in their careers, and become more self-sufficient.

Boosts confidence and self-esteem: As individuals work on themselves and achieve their goals, they develop a sense of confidence and self-esteem. This positive self-image allows individuals to take on new challenges and push themselves outside their comfort zone. With an enhanced level of confidence, individuals are more likely to succeed in their personal and professional endeavors.

Promotes adaptability and flexibility: Continuous self-improvement prepares individuals to adapt to changes and challenges in their personal and professional lives. By constantly learning and evolving, individuals become more flexible and open-minded, making it easier for them to navigate through unexpected situations. This quality is highly valued in the workplace, where individuals who are adaptable and flexible are more likely to thrive.

Fosters personal growth and fulfillment: Continuous self-improvement is a lifelong journey that allows individuals to discover their true potential. By setting goals and working towards achieving them, individuals can grow and become a better version of themselves. This process also promotes a sense of fulfillment and satisfaction, as individuals see the tangible results of their efforts.

Builds resilience: Inevitably, life presents challenges and setbacks that can be difficult to deal with. However, individuals who engage in continuous self-improvement build resilience, which is the ability to bounce back from these challenges. By developing coping mechanisms and a positive mindset, individuals can overcome obstacles and emerge stronger and more resilient.

Improves relationships: Continuous self-improvement not only benefits individuals but also the people around them. By becoming a better version of themselves, individuals can improve their relationships with family, friends, and colleagues. They can learn to communicate effectively, resolve conflicts, and be more empathetic, which leads to healthier and more fulfilling relationships.

Conclusively, continuous self-improvement is crucial for personal and professional growth. It allows individuals to become more self-aware, develop new skills, increase their confidence, and foster personal growth. By continuously working on oneself, individuals can overcome challenges, achieve their goals, and live a more fulfilling life. Therefore, it is essential to make self-improvement a priority and commit to it in all aspects of life.

Why it is crucial to keep striving for personal growth?

First and foremost, personal growth allows us to expand our horizons and break out of our comfort zones. When we challenge ourselves and push beyond our limitations, we open ourselves up to new experiences, opportunities, and perspectives. It helps us to develop a growth mindset, where we see failures and setbacks as opportunities for learning and improvement rather than obstacles. By continuously striving for personal growth, we learn to embrace change and adapt to new situations, making us more resilient and better equipped to face any challenges that come our way.

Moreover, personal growth leads to an increase in self-awareness and self-discovery. It allows us to reflect on our thoughts, behaviors, and beliefs and identify areas where we can improve. This self-reflection helps us in understanding ourselves better and enables us to build a stronger sense of self. As we become more self-aware, we gain a better understanding of our strengths, weaknesses, values, and goals, which ultimately leads to personal growth and fulfillment.

Furthermore, personal growth plays a significant role in our personal and professional relationships. As we grow and evolve, we become better at communication, empathy, and understanding others. This leads to more fulfilling and meaningful relationships with friends, family, and colleagues. Additionally, personal growth also enables us to set healthy boundaries for ourselves and foster healthy relationships based on mutual respect and support.

In today's world, where change is constant, keeping up with personal growth is crucial for one's success and happiness. Personal growth allows us to continuously learn and develop new skills, making us more adaptable to the constantly evolving job market. It also opens doors for personal and professional opportunities, leading to emotional and financial stability. Furthermore, personal growth allows us to set and achieve our goals, leading to a sense of accomplishment and satisfaction.

Ways to continuously improve oneself

Continuous improvement is the key to personal growth and development. It allows us to become the best version of ourselves and reach our full potential. However, it can be challenging to know where to start or how to continue on this journey. Here are some ways to continuously improve oneself:

Set clear and achievable goals: The first step in any improvement journey is to have a clear understanding of your goals. Set specific, measurable, and achievable goals that you can work towards. This will provide you with a sense of direction and motivation to keep going.

Learn new things: Constantly learning and expanding your knowledge is crucial for personal growth. Attend workshops, seminars, or enroll in courses that interest you. Read books, watch educational videos, and listen to podcasts. Learning new things will keep your mind sharp and open up new opportunities for growth.

Reflect and self-assess: Take time to reflect on your actions, behaviors, and thoughts. Self-assessment is essential to understand your strengths, weaknesses, and areas that require improvement. Ask for feedback from trusted friends or mentors to gain a better understanding of yourself.

Practice self-discipline: Self-discipline is the ability to control your impulses and stay focused on your goals. It is a vital skill to cultivate for continuous self-improvement. Set a daily routine, stick to it, and eliminate any distractions that may hinder your progress.

Step out of your comfort zone: Growth and improvement often occur when we step out of our comfort zone. Take on new challenges, try new things, and don't be afraid to make mistakes. Embrace discomfort and use it as an opportunity to learn and grow.

Embrace a growth mindset: A growth mindset is the belief that your abilities and intelligence can be developed through dedication and hard work. Embrace this mindset and believe in your potential for growth and improvement. Don't let setbacks discourage you, but rather use them as learning experiences.

Prioritize self-care: Taking care of yourself is essential for personal growth and improvement. Make time for activities that promote your physical, mental, and emotional well-being. Get enough sleep, exercise regularly, eat healthy, and practice mindfulness.

Surround yourself with positive influences: The people we spend the most time with can greatly impact our mindset and behavior. Surround yourself with positive, supportive, and inspiring individuals who motivate you to be the best version of yourself.

Track your progress: Keeping track of your progress is crucial to stay motivated and see how far you've come. It can also help identify areas that require more attention and improvement.

Be patient and consistent: Remember that personal growth takes time and consistency. Be patient with yourself, celebrate your progress, and keep pushing forward despite any obstacles or setbacks.

Continuous self-improvement is a lifelong journey that requires dedication, self-reflection, and a growth mindset. By implementing these strategies and making them a part of your daily routine, you can continuously improve yourself and become the best version of yourself.

Seeking guidance and mentorship

Seeking guidance and mentorship is an important aspect of personal and professional growth. It is the process of seeking advice, support, and guidance from someone who is more experienced and knowledgeable in a particular area. This can be a teacher, coach, senior colleague, or even a family member or friend.

The journey of seeking guidance and mentorship begins with a realization that we cannot do everything on our own. It is a sign of strength and maturity to recognize our own limitations and seek help from someone who has been through similar experiences and can offer valuable insights and advice.

One of the greatest benefits of seeking guidance and mentorship is gaining access to a wealth of knowledge and experience. Mentors have been through the struggles and challenges that we are currently facing, and their guidance can help us navigate through them more confidently and efficiently. They can offer different perspectives and help us see things in a new light, which can be incredibly valuable in decision-making and problem-solving.

Moreover, a mentor can also provide emotional support and motivation. In times of self-doubt and uncertainty, a mentor can offer words of encouragement and remind us of our strengths, pushing us to reach our full potential. They can also be a source of accountability, helping us stay on track and focused on our goals.

Seeking guidance and mentorship also allows for personal growth and development. By learning from someone who has achieved success in their own life, we can gain valuable skills and knowledge that can help us in our own journey. They can also provide guidance on how to improve our weaknesses and build upon our strengths.

Another significant benefit of seeking guidance and mentorship is the opportunity for networking. A mentor can introduce us to their network and open doors that we otherwise wouldn't have access to. This can be crucial in career growth and development, as well as in building meaningful relationships.

However, seeking guidance and mentorship is not a one-sided relationship. It requires dedication, commitment, and a willingness to learn and improve. It is a two-way street, where both parties need to invest time and effort for it to be successful. It is also essential to choose a mentor carefully, someone we trust and admire, whose values align with our own.

Benefits of having a mentor or coach

Having a mentor or coach can bring many benefits to both personal and professional development. Here are some of the key benefits of having a mentor or coach:

Guidance and Support: A mentor or coach can provide valuable guidance and support in navigating various aspects of life, whether it be career, relationships, or personal goals. They can offer their experience, expertise, and insights to help an individual make more informed decisions and overcome challenges.

Accountability: Having a mentor or coach can also help an individual stay accountable for their goals and actions. They can provide regular check-ins and hold the individual accountable for their progress, keeping them motivated and on track towards their goals.

Expanded Network: A mentor or coach can introduce an individual to their network of connections, opening up opportunities for professional growth and development. This can also help expand an individual's own network, creating potential for new collaborations and partnerships.

Personalized Guidance: Unlike a classroom or traditional learning environment, having a mentor or coach allows for personalized guidance that caters to an individual's specific needs and goals. They can provide tailored advice and strategies that are relevant to an individual's unique situation.

Challenging Limiting Beliefs: Mentors and coaches can help individuals identify and challenge limiting beliefs that may be holding them back from reaching their full potential. They can provide a different perspective and help an individual break through barriers and make positive changes.

Faster Progression: With a mentor or coach's guidance and support, an individual can make faster progress towards their goals. They can provide insights and strategies that can help an individual achieve their objectives in a more efficient and effective way.

Personal Growth: A mentor or coach can also aid in an individual's personal growth and development. They can provide constructive feedback and help an individual identify areas for improvement, enabling them to become more self-aware and make positive changes.

Learn from Someone Else's Experience: Having a mentor or coach means learning from someone who has already been through similar experiences. They can share their successes, failures, and lessons learned, providing valuable insights and knowledge that an individual can apply to their own journey.

Motivation and Inspiration: A mentor or coach can serve as a source of motivation and inspiration, especially during difficult times. They can offer encouragement and support, reminding an individual of their potential and helping them stay motivated to achieve their goals.

Long-Term Benefits: The benefits of having a mentor or coach can have a lasting impact. The skills, knowledge, and habits an individual learns from their mentor or coach can continue to benefit them throughout their lives, helping them achieve greater success and fulfillment.

How to find and learn from mentors

Finding and learning from mentors is a valuable and impactful way to grow personally and professionally. Mentors are experienced individuals who have achieved success in their respective fields and can provide guidance, knowledge, and support to those looking to further their own development. A mentor can offer valuable insights, share their own experiences, and provide honest feedback to help you reach your goals and navigate challenges.

Here are some steps to find and learn from mentors:

Set clear goals: Before seeking a mentor, it is important to have a clear understanding of your objectives and what you hope to gain from the mentoring relationship. Identify the areas in which you would like to improve and the skills you want to learn. This will help you find a mentor who has the expertise and knowledge you need to achieve your goals.

Build a network: One of the best ways to find mentors is by building a strong professional network. Attend networking events, seminars, and conferences related to your field of interest. This will provide you with opportunities to meet experienced professionals who can potentially become your mentors. Use social media platforms like LinkedIn to connect with people in your industry and expand your network.

Be proactive and approach potential mentors: Don't be afraid to approach individuals you admire and ask them to be your mentor. You can reach out to them through email, LinkedIn, or in person. Be polite, respectful, and clear about your objectives and how the mentorship can benefit both of you. Keep in mind that not everyone you approach will agree to be your mentor, and that's okay. Be persistent and keep reaching out to other potential mentors until you find the right fit.

Seek mentorship from different sources: Mentors don't necessarily have to be in your immediate network or even in the same field as you. Consider seeking mentorship from people outside your industry who have skills or experiences that align with your goals. You can also look for mentorship from online communities, professional groups, or even through educational programs.

Be committed and open to feedback: Once you've found a mentor, it is essential to be dedicated and respectful of their time and expertise. Be open to constructive criticism and feedback, and actively work on implementing their suggestions. Remember that the mentor is investing their time and knowledge in you, so it is important to show gratitude and make the most of the mentorship.

Develop a learning plan: To make the most out of your mentorship, it is helpful to develop a structured learning plan. This can include setting goals, identifying specific skills and knowledge you want to acquire, and creating a timeline for achieving them. Your mentor can provide guidance and support in developing this plan and holding you accountable.

Be a good mentee: A successful mentor-mentee relationship is a two-way street. While your mentor is invested in your growth, it is also important for you to be a good mentee. This means being reliable, respectful of their time, actively listening to their advice, and being open to learning and trying new things.

In conclusion, finding and learning from mentors can greatly benefit your personal and professional growth. By setting clear goals, building a network, and being proactive in seeking mentorship, you can find the right mentor who can guide you towards success. Remember to be committed, open to feedback, and develop a structured learning plan to make the most out of this valuable relationship. With the guidance and support of a mentor, you can gain valuable insights and achieve your goals faster.

Celebrating and learning from failures and successes

Failure and success are two sides of the same coin on the journey towards achieving one's goals and dreams. They are inseparable and equally important in the learning process. While success brings joy and boosts confidence, failure often brings disappointment and a sense of defeat. However, both outcomes offer valuable lessons and opportunities for growth and improvement.

Celebrating successes is crucial as it validates one's efforts and hard work. It serves as a reminder that one is capable of achieving their goals and motivates them to strive for more. It also allows for reflection on what went right and can serve as a blueprint for future success. Celebrating success can also inspire and motivate others, creating a ripple effect of positivity.

On the other hand, failure teaches us valuable lessons that can be applied to future endeavors. It shows us what went wrong and presents an opportunity to learn from our mistakes. Celebrating failure can be challenging, but it is essential to create a healthy mindset. By embracing failure as a natural part of the learning process, we can shift our perspective and see it as a stepping stone towards success.

Learning from both failures and successes also requires introspection and self-awareness. It is essential to understand why something worked or didn't work and how we can improve in the future. Taking the time to reflect on both outcomes helps to identify patterns and areas for growth. This can lead to personal development and progress towards achieving our goals.

It is also important to surround ourselves with a support system that celebrates both successes and failures. It is natural to lean towards those who praise our successes, but it is equally important to have people who will support us through our failures and offer constructive criticism. This creates a safe space for growth and learning, where we can openly discuss our achievements and setbacks without fear of judgment.

Both failure and success are integral parts of the learning process. We should celebrate our successes to acknowledge our hard work and accomplishments and learn from our failures to grow and improve. By doing so, we can create a positive mindset and support system that will guide us on our journey towards achieving our goals.

Understanding the importance of reflection and learning from experiences

Reflection is the act of looking back on past experiences, reflecting on what happened, and making sense of it in order to gain new insights and understanding. It is an important process that allows individuals to learn from their experiences and grow both personally and professionally.

One of the key benefits of reflection is that it helps individuals to gain a deeper understanding of themselves and how they perceive the world around them. By taking the time to reflect on their thoughts, emotions, and actions, individuals can identify their strengths, weaknesses, and areas for improvement. This self-awareness allows for personal growth and development, leading to more effective decision-making and goal setting.

Reflection also allows individuals to learn from their successes and failures. By reflecting on what went well and what didn't go well, individuals can identify patterns and behaviors that contribute to their success or hinder their progress. This self-reflection can then inform future actions and strategies, leading to more successful outcomes.

Moreover, reflection promotes continuous learning. By constantly reflecting on experiences, individuals are able to identify new knowledge and skills that can be applied in future situations. This leads to a deeper understanding of oneself and the world, as well as a more adaptable and flexible mindset.

In addition, reflection can also lead to improved relationships and communication. By reflecting on interactions and experiences with others, individuals can gain a better understanding of their own behavior and how it affects those around them. This can improve communication and relationships, as individuals become more self-aware and better able to adapt their communication style to meet the needs of others.

Overall, reflection is an essential tool for personal and professional growth. It allows individuals to gain new insights and understanding, learn from their experiences, and continuously improve themselves. By taking the time to reflect, individuals can build self-awareness, improve their decision-making, and foster positive relationships, ultimately leading to a more fulfilling and successful life.

How to use failures and successes as opportunities for growth

Failures and successes are two sides of the same coin. While successes bring a sense of achievement and satisfaction, failures come with disappointment and often, a fear of trying again. However, it is essential to understand that both failures and successes are vital opportunities for personal growth and development.

Failures can be one of the toughest experiences in life, as they often shatter our confidence and bring a feeling of defeat. If not handled well, failures can also lead to self-doubt and fear of taking risks. However, failures provide the ultimate opportunity for growth as they force us to reflect on our mistakes and weaknesses. Through failures, we can identify areas that require improvement and learn from our mistakes. It is rightly said, "Failure is not falling down, but refusing to get up." Similarly, failures are not the end; instead, they are stepping stones in our journey towards success and growth.

One of the biggest lessons that failures teach us is resilience. It is easy to give up and accept defeat, but failures push us to keep going and try again. They provide us with the opportunity to develop a growth mindset, where we see challenges as opportunities to learn and grow. As we overcome failures and move forward, we become more resilient and better equipped to face obstacles in the future.

In addition to resilience, failures also help us develop humility and self-awareness. When we fail, we are forced to acknowledge that we are not perfect and that we have room for improvement. This realization allows us to step back and reflect on our actions, thoughts, and behaviors, leading to self-awareness. It helps us identify our strengths and weaknesses, allowing us to work on improving ourselves.

On the other hand, successes are equally important for growth and development. It is natural to feel proud and satisfied with our achievements. However, just like failures, successes also offer opportunities for growth. We can learn a lot from our successes, such as the importance of hard work, determination, and perseverance. Successes give us the confidence to take on new challenges and push ourselves further.

Another crucial aspect of successes is that they provide us with a sense of fulfillment and motivation. As we achieve our goals, we feel a sense of purpose and direction in life. This motivates us to continue striving for more significant achievements and success, leading to further growth and development. Furthermore, successes also help us understand our strengths, talents, and abilities, allowing us to make informed decisions about our future goals and aspirations.

Chapter 12
Conclusion

Recap of the rules of success

The journey to achieving success can often seem daunting and overwhelming. With so many factors at play and different definitions of success for individuals, it can be challenging to determine the right path to follow. However, there are certain overarching principles or rules that can guide one towards success, regardless of their goals or aspirations. These rules serve as a blueprint for success and can help individuals navigate through challenges and setbacks on their journey. Let's take a closer look at some of the most effective rules for achieving success:

Believe in yourself: The first and most crucial rule for success is to have faith in yourself. Believe that you have the talent, skills, and determination to achieve your goals. Without self-belief, it is easy to get discouraged or give up altogether when faced with obstacles. Believe in your abilities and keep a positive mindset, no matter what challenges come your way.

Set clear, achievable goals: An essential aspect of achieving success is to set clear, specific, and achievable goals. Vague or undefined goals can lead to confusion and lack of direction. When setting your goals, be specific about what you want to achieve, and make sure they are attainable. They should also be time-bound, giving you a deadline to work towards. This will help you stay focused and motivated as you work towards your goals.

Develop a plan and be disciplined: Having a plan or roadmap to guide your actions is crucial for success. A plan will help you stay organized, motivated, and on track towards your goals. However, it is important to develop a plan that is flexible enough to accommodate unexpected challenges and changes. Along with a plan, it is also essential to cultivate discipline in your actions. This means being consistent, committed, and accountable for your efforts towards success.

Learn from failures and setbacks: One of the most significant obstacles to success is fear of failure. However, failure is a natural part of any journey, and it is often said that it is the first step towards success. Instead of being discouraged by failures and setbacks, use them as learning opportunities. Analyze what went wrong, and use that knowledge to improve and grow. Remember that every failure brings you one step closer to success.

Surround yourself with positive influences: We are the average of the people we spend the most time with. Therefore, it is crucial to surround yourself with positive influences who support, encourage, and inspire you on your journey to success. Stay away from negative influences and people who bring you down. Surrounding yourself with like-minded individuals who have achieved success or are working towards it can also motivate and guide you towards your goals.

Prioritize personal growth: Success is not just about achieving external goals; it is also about personal growth and development. Continuously striving to improve and enhance your skills, knowledge, and abilities can give you a competitive edge and open doors for new opportunities. Invest in yourself through learning, self-reflection, and personal development to not only achieve success but sustain it in the long run.

Be persistent and determined: Achieving success does not happen overnight. It takes consistent effort, determination, and persistence to overcome challenges and reach your goals. It is normal to face obstacles and setbacks on the path to success, but what sets successful people apart is their ability to persevere and push through despite the odds. Never give up on your dreams and keep moving forward with determination.

In conclusion, success is a journey, not a destination. It is a result of consistent effort, determination, and following these essential rules. Remember to always believe in yourself, set clear and achievable goals, have a plan, learn from failures, surround yourself with positive influences, prioritize personal growth, and stay persistent and determined. With these rules in mind, you can navigate through challenges and ultimately achieve success in any aspect of your life.

Encouragement to implement these rules in daily life

Implementing rules of success in daily life is crucial in achieving personal growth and fulfillment. Whether in career, relationships, or personal development, following these rules can lead to remarkable improvements in one's life. However, it is common for individuals to struggle with incorporating these rules into their daily routine. This is where encouragement plays a significant role.

First and foremost, encouragement helps build motivation and drive in individuals to put these rules into practice. With the hectic and demanding nature of modern-day living, it is easy to get bogged down and lose sight of our goals. Encouragement acts as a constant reminder to stay focused and dedicated to following these rules even when faced with challenges and setbacks. It helps individuals stay committed to their personal growth journey, even on days when they feel demotivated.

Furthermore, encouragement serves as a source of support and inspiration. When individuals feel encouraged, they are more likely to take risks, try new things, and step out of their comfort zone. This is crucial in implementing these rules of success, which often involve taking on new challenges and breaking old habits. Encouragement from others can push individuals to embrace change and push beyond their limits, leading to personal growth and development.

Incorporating these rules of success in daily life can also improve one's self-confidence. When individuals see themselves actively implementing these rules and achieving their goals, it boosts their self-belief and self-worth. This, in turn, encourages them to continue striving for success and not give up in the face of obstacles. With a positive self-image, individuals are more likely to continue implementing these rules, leading to a cycle of growth and achievement.

Moreover, encouragement can come in various forms, which makes it adaptable and accessible to everyone. It can come from mentors, friends, family, or even oneself. A simple statement of "you can do this" can make all the difference in motivating someone to take action towards success. Encouragement can also come through positive affirmations and self-talk, serving as a constant reminder of one's potential and ability to succeed.

Encouragement also promotes a growth mindset, which is essential in implementing these rules of success. A growth mindset is the belief that one's abilities and intelligence can be developed through effort and dedication. With this mindset, individuals are more likely to view challenges as opportunities for growth and learning, rather than setbacks. This encourages individuals to persist in implementing these rules, even when faced with difficulties.

Finally, encouragement can also create a positive and supportive environment for personal growth and success. When individuals are surrounded by individuals who support and encourage them, it creates a sense of accountability and motivation.

This encourages individuals to stay on track and continue implementing these rules, especially when faced with distractions or temptations to give up.

Final thoughts on achieving success.

Achieving success is a journey that looks different for everyone. Some may define success as wealth and material possessions, while others may view it as achieving personal goals and finding inner fulfillment. Whatever the definition may be, one thing is certain: success takes hard work, dedication, and persistence.

Throughout life, individuals encounter challenges, obstacles, and setbacks that may hinder their path to success. However, it is important to remember that these struggles are necessary for growth and development. The road to success is not a straight line, but rather a series of ups and downs that can shape a person's character and teach valuable lessons.

In order to achieve success, one must have a clear vision and set achievable goals. It is important to constantly reassess and adjust these goals as one progresses on their journey. This allows for growth, improvement, and staying on track towards the desired outcome.

Another crucial aspect of achieving success is developing a strong work ethic. Success does not come easily and requires hard work, determination, and consistency. It is important to have a strong sense of discipline and commitment towards one's goals. This may mean sacrificing leisure time, taking risks, and pushing oneself out of their comfort zone, but the end result is well worth it.

In addition, it is essential to surround oneself with positive influences and a supportive community. Success is not achieved in isolation, and having a network of family, friends, and mentors who believe in one's abilities can greatly contribute to one's success. These individuals can offer guidance, motivation, and a sense of accountability.

Furthermore, it is important to have a positive mindset and not let failures or setbacks define one's journey. Failure is a natural part of the process and should be embraced as a learning opportunity. It is through failures that one can learn valuable lessons, make necessary adjustments, and ultimately grow.

Lastly, it is crucial to remember that success does not equate to perfection. It is important to celebrate small victories along the way and not become too focused on the end goal. Enjoying the journey and being grateful for the progress made is a fundamental aspect of achieving success.

In conclusion, success is a combination of hard work, determination, resilience, and a positive mindset. It is a continuous journey where one must constantly reassess and adjust their goals, surround themselves with supportive influences, and stay focused on their vision. Embracing failures, having a strong work ethic, and being grateful for the progress made are key factors in achieving success. Ultimately, success is not a destination, but rather a series of ongoing efforts towards personal growth and fulfillment.